You are to be commended for ma  rkle
throughout the book.... I agree witl h is
weak because we are not founded o tles,
nor is the Nation.

ıford
Co-founder, Elijah House Ministries, Inc.
Author of *The Elijah Task*

Ron Campbell is one of the few prophetic messengers in the apostolic movement today who I believe is called to, and functions in, the office of prophet. *The Prophetic Path* is a three-stranded cord: the personal journey of a New Testament prophet, a journey of knowledge and insight into God's written word, and a journey into rhema revelation. Ron is a prophetic pioneer who unashamedly and courageously proclaims direction and correction as the prophets of old, and exhorts and edifies as the prophets of today. This book is a tour de force and a must read for all who love Christ, his church, and his kingdom.

~ Apostle John P. Kelly, Th.D
Convener International Coalition of Apostolic Leaders

Rather than just sharing victorious insights, Ron Campbell offers many humbling mistakes which are the stuff of deep learning for the Reader. The result is a window into prophetic ministry that encourages people both to receive prophetic words and to step out themselves to listen for God's voice. Very rare among contemporary prophets, Ron also has a commitment to pay the heavy price required to speak hard words instead of superficial fluff, but to do it in a compassionate and gentle way.

~ The Rt. Rev. Dr. Bill Atwood
Bishop of The International Diocese
ACNA Suffragan Bishop for Int'l Affairs
All Saints Cathedral Diocese
Nairobi Anglican Church of Kenya

Ron Campbell was summoned by the Lord and sent to the nations. *The Prophetic Path* reveals his journey and will inspire you to know the Lord and prevail. "[F]rom a far-off land, [I summoned] a man to fulfill my purpose" Isaiah 46:11.

~ Charles (Tiny) Lynn
Author of *Why the Nations Rage*
Speaker, Diplomatic Humanitarian

The Prophetic Path is a comprehensive narrative, seamlessly written, and laced with right insights born of years of testing, seasoning, agonizing, wrestling, warring, and winning in the fight against the powers of darkness. As God has used Ron Campbell in so many significant ways, his is a story of how, when there is a fresh in-breaking of the kingdom of God, there is also a further debilitating effect on the kingdom of Darkness. This work is one you will want to read again and again and use as a ready reference in your library of resources to be energized, sustained, and motivated, as you become part of a vanguard prophetic company. It is desperately needed.

~ Dr. Mark J. Chironna
Church On The Living Edge
Mark Chironna Ministries
Longwood, Florida

The Prophetic Path is a manual, a template, and a pattern for these times in our nation. Ron clearly and uniquely defines the walk of a prophet. All he lived and survived was preparation to teach, train and lead a prophetic people in these last days. I fully charge every modern-day prophet to make this book your roadmap.

~ Dianne Palmer
Dianne Palmer Ministries
Secret Place prophetic music CD

Every believer needs to read this book, especially with the re-emergence of the apostles and prophets. Ron Campbell is uncommonly transparent. I highly recommend it!

~ Terry Moore, Senior Pastor
Sojourn Church, Carrollton, TX

The Prophetic Path challenges and inspires, as Ron Campbell shares his personal journey and witness to the place, power, and purpose of the prophetic needed in the Body of Christ today. Most of all you'll learn the joy of walking with a listening ear to heaven to bring the blessings of heaven to earth.

~ Dr. Walter Fletcher
Apostolic Regional Leader
Dallas, Texas

The Prophetic Path

a practical guide for New Testament prophets

RON CAMPBELL

with *New York Times* bestselling author

RON BRACKIN

Foreword by Bishop Joseph Garlington

ISBN-10: 0-692-79296-1
ISBN-13: 978-0-692-79296-4

Sound the Trumpet Publications
PO Box 188
Grapevine, TX 76099
www.soundthetrumpet.org

COVER: Josh Andrew Brown Design, www.joshandrewbrown.com.

COVER PHOTO: 31,000 square mile Namib Desert, Namibia, where Ron Campbell trained in the military.

"Do not think that I came to abolish the Law or the Prophets."

~ Matthew 5:17

acknowledgments

To Melanie, Kirsty-Lee, Jessica, and Gemme, as well as Kayla, Chloe, Austin, Levi, Sebastian, Sophia, and Amelia, as well as Benji. We have had an interesting journey. Thank you!

To Ron and Annie Brackin. We have worked so wonderfully to create this phenomenal work!

To Vernon and Betty Fisher, who walked alongside me in the beginning of my journey. I am blessed that the Lord chose you to direct my path with light and truth.

To Peter Van Niekerk and Peter Bellinghan, true friends who taught me about God's kingdom.

To prophet Roger Teale, thank you for wisdom and guidance, as well as great friendship.

To apostle Bob Terrell, you made a way where there was no way. I am so grateful for your wisdom.

Last but not least, to Toblerone and Ragusa Swiss chocolates. You comforted me in the wee hours while I wrote this book. Thank you!

contents

foreword

"I was neither a prophet nor the son of a prophet, but I was a shepherd, and I also took care of sycamore-fig trees. But the Lord took me from tending the flock and said to me, 'Go, prophesy to my people Israel.'"[1]

Those who have concluded that the office of the prophet and the gift of prophecy are no longer necessary need only look at the current state of the church to see that they are urgently needed.

I met Prophet Ron Campbell more than ten years ago at a small conference in northern New Jersey. I had only heard about him through my associates and that he had impacted their churches.

He was unassuming and modest in his bearing. His demeanor gave no hint of the power and accuracy of his prophetic ministry. He said that he had looked forward to getting to meet me, and I said the same thing.

Throughout the weekend, as we got to know one another better, we realized it was a divine appointment. We connected, exchanged contact information, and promised to stay in touch with each other.

We connected years later at a significant team meeting in Texas, where someone informed him he could never have a relationship with me! Over the years, Ron has suffered rejection from significant leaders in the body of Christ, and this seemed to be one more. I was unaware of this event until years later and was deeply grieved.

Nevertheless, through an act of obedience, Ron reached out to me

---

[1] Amos 7:14-15.

i

with a word from the Lord that I desperately needed. We reconnected, and as the saying goes, the rest is history.

There is also a saying that, "Those who can, do; those who can't, teach." While not axiomatic, it is too often the case in the kingdom of God. The body of Christ is in desperate need of prophetic voices—men and women who will lift their voices and address both kingdom and national issues.

But these voices must be authentic and trustworthy. Accountable, not "lone rangers." Prophets who have been tried and proven and who have emerged better, not bitter.

> For You have tried us, O God; You have refined us as silver is refined. You brought us into the net; You laid an oppressive burden upon our loins. You made men ride over our heads; We went through fire and through water, yet You brought us out into *a place of* abundance.[2]

The Josephs, Daniels, Nehemiahs, Esthers, and Sarahs were all godly people who came through God's purifying furnace prepared for the tasks ahead of them.

Charles Simpson, a pioneer of the charismatic renewal movement, said "The pathway to ruling is protected and guarded by problems that only men of Spirit-given wisdom and godly character can solve."

I have watched Ron Campbell make a determined effort to solve kingdom problems God's way.

The Prophetic Path is the distillation of years of walking with and listening to God. I pray that it will inspire and encourage budding prophets to seek mentoring from seasoned prophetic voices that have been tried in fire.

I commend this fresh word to the many who are seeking to know

---

[2] Psalm 66:10-12 NASB.

more about prophecy and the prophetic.

The prophetic is not archaic, not part of a bygone dispensation. It was, and continues to be, the will and plan of God.

"Would that all the Lord's people were prophets, that the Lord would put His Spirit upon them!"[3]

"Now I wish that you all spoke in tongues, but *even* more that you would prophesy."[4]

~ Bishop Joseph L. Garlington, Sr.
Senior Pastor of Covenant Church of Pittsburgh
Presiding Bishop
Reconciliation! An International Network of Churches and Ministries

---

[3] Numbers 11:29 NASB.
[4] 1 Corinthians 14:5 NASB.

introduction

At 2,722 feet (twice the height of New York's Empire State Building) the Burj Khalifa skyscraper in Dubai is currently the tallest building in the world. To support its half-million-ton weight, and to compensate for loose to medium dense sands overlying weak to very weak sandstone and siltstone, requires a foundation of 192 bored piles, 5 feet in diameter and approximately 164 feet deep, beneath a 12-foot-thick raft foundation.[5]

Like a towering skyscraper, the church is only as strong as its foundation.

✸ Consequently, you are no longer foreigners and strangers, but fellow citizens with God's people and also members of his household, *built on the foundation of the apostles and prophets*, with Christ Jesus himself as the chief cornerstone. In him the whole building is joined together and rises to become a holy temple in the Lord. And in him you too are being built together to become a dwelling in which God lives by his Spirit.[6]

But what if the church, Christ's family and visible presence on earth, is built upon a different foundation?

Much of the post-apostolic church, extending even until today, has rejected the validity of New Testament apostles and prophets, arguing that they are no longer needed and building instead upon a foundation of pastors and teachers. But the Chief Architect never

---

[5] Post, Randy, "Foundations and Geotechnic Engineering for the Burj Dubai – World's Tallest Building," GeoPrac.Net: geological, geotechnical engineering news, articles, community, 04 January 2010.
[6] Ephesians 2:19-22, emphasis added.

1

designed pastors and teachers to serve as "load-bearing walls." He intended the burden to be more widely distributed.

> So Christ himself gave the apostles, the prophets, the evangelists, the pastors and teachers, to equip his people for works of service, so that the body of Christ may be built up until we all reach unity in the faith and in the knowledge of the Son of God and become mature, attaining to the whole measure of the fullness of Christ.[7]

Without the apostles and the prophets, how can the body of Christ be built up? How can we reach unity in the faith and in the knowledge of the Son of God? How will the church mature? How can Christians hope to attain to the whole measure of the fullness of Christ? And how can an immature church serve as salt and light to the nations?

Ignoring two of the five-fold offices is a little like removing a couple of sparkplugs and expecting your car to run efficiently.

Thankfully, while the church may deviate from the plan, God never does. And the Holy Spirit is restoring the apostles and prophets to his church. He is recreating us all to reflect Jesus, until we—the earthly embodiment of Christ—are able to say to the world, as Jesus said to Philip, "Anyone who has seen me has seen the Father."[8]

While *The Prophetic Path* makes no boast of being encyclopedic, it does offer a starting point, along with some fundamental principles and practical guidelines. And while it is written chiefly to God's New Testament prophets, it applies to the rest of the body of Christ as well.

"I wish that all the LORD's people were prophets," Moses said, "and that the LORD would put his Spirit on them!"[9]

God responded to that wish.

---

[7] Ephesians 4:11-13.
[8] John 14:9.
[9] Numbers 11:29.

2

> In the last days, God says, I will pour out my Spirit on *all people*. Your sons and daughters will prophesy, your young men will see visions, your old men will dream dreams. Even on my servants, both men and women, I will pour out my Spirit in those days, and they will prophesy.[10]

And it came to pass at Pentecost.[11]

It is important to understand, however, that while prophecy is available to all believers, not everyone who prophesies is a prophet, any more than everyone who has an M.D. is a brain surgeon. Prophecy is a gift; the office of a prophet is a call.

I was called down a road full of potholes and broken glass.

nightmare

My prophetic path began in Johannesburg, South Africa, in 1957. And it nearly killed me.

My father was as hard as the steel industry that put food on our table and tempered by a losing battle with alcoholism. A retired naval officer, he was a harsh disciplinarian. The chores he required of us were Dickensian, straight out of a Victorian workhouse.

After I was born, he sent me to an orphanage with my sisters while he and our mother tried to fix their marriage. My grandfather took me out of the orphanage to live with him for a while. Then he died, and my parents brought me home. Nothing had changed. My father was still a brutal, merciless man who beat me out of whim and habit.

My high school years were spent in Elsburg, a mining town outside of Germiston that boasts the biggest rail shunting[12] yard in the southern hemisphere. Most of the people in town were Afrikaners

---

[10] Acts 2:17-18, emphasis added.
[11] Acts 2:2-8.
[12] Called "switching" in the United States, shunting is the process of sorting and assembling specifically purposed rolling stock (train cars) into the required formation before hitching them to their locomotive(s).

3

(Dutch descendants), but the Campbells are Scots, which were lumped together with the English and made life hell for me.

Afrikaners and Englishmen hated each other, bad blood that originated with the Second Anglo-Boer War (1899-1902), when the British murdered Afrikaner families and destroyed their farms and livestock. The feud was further aggravated during the Second World War when the British forced Afrikaners into internment camps because of their German sympathies. Many died there.[13]

I had to attend an Africaans school, where I and my English friends were brutalized every day.

Going to school became like a military maneuver. The Afrikaners hunted us in packs, beating their victims or burning their genitalia with dry ice. Each day, we tried to work out where the enemy waited for us.

Between home and school, I had no refuge. I grew angry, hard, and merciless. My friends and I formed a band to defend ourselves, and school became like a daily rumble between street gangs.

Each visit to my home by the police turned into another excuse for my father to beat me until I was just about broken.

When I was twelve, I stole my father's car and drove five hours to Durban, intending to stow away on a ship and go to America. I became increasingly violent and dangerous and tried many times to kill myself.

Finally, a few months after my sixteenth birthday, my father decided to send me to the military. "Going to the navy will make a man of you," he said. "Don't come back until it has!"[14]

I was taken to South Africa's largest naval training station in

---

[13] The amazing history of South Africa is dramatically and accurately portrayed in James A. Michener's *The Covenant*.

[14] Years later, my mother and father gave their lives to the Lord. My father and I were reconciled before he passed away in 1987.

Saldanha Bay, three hours from Cape Town where I completed boot camp.

the prelude

In June 1976, I was assigned to the flagship SAS President Kruger.[15] We were to participate in an international naval review—a fleet of fifty-three vessels from twenty-two nations—to celebrate America's Bicentennial, which also made us the first South African naval vessel ever to visit the United States.

South Africa at this time was about halfway through a bloody border war with Angola and Namibia, with the United Nations squarely against us. Relations between South Africa and America were at an all-time low.

When we reached New York, our multinational fleet was joined by magnificent tall ships and surrounded by countless small vessels with horns blaring, sails flapping, and bells ringing.

Once the tall ships sailed by, we all docked in New York Harbor, and thousands of sailors poured into Manhattan on liberty.[16] For the next week, everything was free for us in the famous Big Apple. We went crazy!

Later that afternoon, I toured Liberty Island with some of my shipmates, while we waited for what promised to be a spectacular fireworks display in the harbor.

I remember standing there, looking at the broken chains at Lady Liberty's feet, and I was overwhelmed by a sense of destiny. I looked out over the Hudson River to Manhattan Island.

Even today, I can't explain what I felt. I was nineteen. All I know is that God spoke to my heart that day, even before I ever heard his voice, and I knew I would be back.

---

[15] Six years after our voyage to America, the 2100-ton, 370-foot frigate sank after colliding with her replenishment ship, SAS Tafelberg in the South Atlantic. Sixteen of the ship's 250 crew members were lost.
[16] Shore leave.

5

On the way home, we spent a week at the Naval Air Station in Charleston, South Carolina and I visited historic sites of the Revolutionary War. As I touched the history of this unique nation, I felt a strange bond that I would not understand for many years, a bond that I all but forgot as my life continued downward.

the encounter

By 1985, a civilian again, I was hopelessly lost. I hated myself and thought my only mission in life was to destroy my enemies and those of my country. My elite military training had taught me that violence was the solution to every problem.

One Sunday night, drunk, I walked through town and came to a movie theater that had lights on inside. This was unusual because everything is closed on church day throughout South Africa. Nevertheless, a movie sounded like a good idea, so I walked in.

But there was no movie, only music. And the auditorium was filled with people dancing and waving their arms in the air.

My first thought was that I had stumbled into a wedding, which meant there would be a bar, so I went in search of a drink. When I couldn't find one, I returned to the back of the auditorium and just stood there, watching and listening. Suddenly, the piano player stopped playing.

"You in the blue shirt," he called out.

I started down the aisle, thinking I had been caught crashing the wedding.

"'Your days of wildness and running around are over,' says the Lord! 'For I have put a bit in your mouth and a bridle upon your head, and I have restrained you.'" I fell to the floor, which really made me mad. I lay there wondering who had tripped me and deciding how I would take revenge on both him and the piano player.

As I lay there, I felt as though I was being crushed. The weight got heavier and heavier and I thought I was going to suffocate. You know how they say people on the brink of death see their whole life flash before their eyes? Well, for me it was true.

No one came to see if I was hurt. They just left me there. I woke up about four in the morning. The theater was dark, so I let myself out the emergency exit.

I returned the following Sunday, and the pastor called me up and prophesied over me.

"I have called you to be a prophet to the nations, and I will take you to the nation where I spoke to your heart at the gateway, the nation that is the apple of my eye."

He asked me if I knew Jesus.

"No," I said, "because I've never met him."

"Would you like to meet him?"

"Yes. Where is he? Bring him here and let me meet him."

Then he asked me to pray with him to repent and ask Jesus to come into my heart. I was confused, but I couldn't resist. The experience was overwhelming. They told me I needed to be water baptized. But I had trouble finding somebody to baptize me because I had a violent reputation and people who knew me stayed well clear of me.

But the Holy Spirit sent a man who I had known in the military. Vernon said the Lord had spoken to him about me and burdened him to pray for me. So he baptized me in water.

Not long after this, the baptism of the Holy Spirit came like fire. I shook for days and spoke in a strange language I didn't understand. But I didn't care. For the first time in my wretched life, I felt alive.

retraining

Vernon discipled me over the next two years and led me through

7

much-needed deliverance, as I continued growing in my faith day by day and believing the Lord. After being baptized in the Holy Spirit, my journey of discovery began in earnest. I became intrigued with the pastor's word about being called as a prophet and wondered how that worked in the modern context. But I could find no one who could teach me about the prophetic path.

I read John Sanford's *Elijah Task*[17] and books by Bill Hamon,[18] seminal works for men and women the Holy Spirit is calling and commissioning as New Testament prophets. I strongly recommend that everyone read them to help build a solid biblical foundation in the prophetic. But I still had questions about how to be led by the Holy Spirit, questions the Lord has answered for me over the past twenty-five years.

> As for you, the anointing you received from him remains in you, and you do not need anyone to teach you. But as his anointing teaches you about all things and as that anointing is real, not counterfeit—just as it has taught you, remain in him.[19]

I started a job as a medical representative for a pharmaceutical company, selling to physicians on South Africa's west coast. That meant I had to drive eight to twelve hours through the Namaqualand and Karoo.

The latter is an arid desert region of great heat and great frosts. The Namaqualand is pretty much the same, except in the spring (August and September in South Africa) when it is suddenly transformed into a dazzling carpet of nearly 4,000 species of flowers, spread out in every direction as far as eye can see.

---

[17] Sanford, John, *The Elijah Task: A Call to Today's Prophets and Intercessors*, Charisma House, 2006.

[18] Dr. Bill Hamon is founder of Christian International School of Theology and its School of the Holy Spirit and author of several books, including *Prophets, Pitfalls and Principles: God's Prophetic People Today* and *Prophets and Personal Prophecy*.

[19] 1 John 2:27. In context, this verse warns the church against false teachers, as opposed to Godly prophets like John Sanford and Bill Hamon. I highlight it apart from its original context because it is an amazing picture of the discipleship relationship between the Holy Spirit and the New Testament prophet.

Vernon encouraged me to pursue the Lord in prayer during my long travel times. As I did, I began to have weird experiences. I thought they were just coincidences at first. When I shared them with Vernon, however, I discovered that I was being directed by the Holy Spirit, which I came to understand as experiential revelation.

Once as I was praying, I had an open vision of a white C130 transport plane, with a big red cross on the tail, taking off and climbing. As the plane banked left, I saw the vapor trail of a heat-seeking missile, then a ball of fire and debris plunging to earth. Stunned, I began to intercede.

After I got home, my sister called to tell me that she and her husband had been transferred to England and that he was going to fly C130s for the Red Cross into Africa. I went to my brother-in-law to warn him about what I saw, but he laughed at me and called me a religious nut case. About eight weeks later, he and five others were shot down over the war zone in Angola, exactly as I had seen in the vision.[20]

> Then I heard the voice of the Lord saying, "Whom
> shall I send? And who will go for us?"
> And I said, "Here am I. Send me!"[21]

---

[20] According to news reports, the Hercules transport plane crashed after taking off from the central city of Kuito. Despite the fact that rebel guerrillas had received shoulder-held antiaircraft Stinger rockets from the United States the year before, UNITA (Union for the Total Independence of Angola) denied targeting the Red Cross plane. UNITA had previously claimed responsibility for shooting down two Angolan-owned TAAG airliners, maintaining that government troops were aboard the flights. (Associated Press, October 15, 1987.) (Brooke, James, "War Status in Angola Is Status Quo," *The New York Times*, December 27, 1987.)

[21] Isaiah 6:8.

CHAPTER ONE
faith

I believe in Christianity as I believe that the Sun has risen, not only because I see it but because by it I see everything else.[22]

~ C.S. Lewis

Before the prophet walked into our meeting, I was a disaster.

Like you, "I was brought forth in [a state of] wickedness; in sin my mother conceived me [and from my beginning I, too, was sinful]."[23]

From birth, I went downhill.

I had nothing but bad examples in my life and emulated them all, got nothing but bad advice and took it all. I learned that I had to fight my way through life, and I got really good at it.

By the time I got saved, my brains were scrambled, my heart was stone, and I woke up and went to bed angry, churning with offenses. Nobody had to tell me I was a failure, and nobody dared to.

For as he thinks within himself, so he is.[24]

In short, I had no concept or hope of ever being a functional human being, whatever that was.

Then I got saved, but little seemed to change. I was told I was now

---

[22] C.S. Lewis, "They Asked for A Paper," in Is Theology Poetry? (London: Geoffrey Bless, 1962), 164-165.
[23] Psalm 51:5 AMP.
[24] Proverbs 23:7 NASB.

a beloved child of God and an overcomer, free of the power of sin. I was even told I had been called to be a prophet. But I couldn't seem to walk in any of it, because I didn't have faith.

That morning, when the prophet came to minister, she called me to the front.

> God has been restraining you! And my goodness, you have pawed the ground like a wild horse tied up.... You are working through bitterness, anger, hurt, and resentment...and you are fed up and frustrated. You have been severely hurt and wounded, and you have seen others run ahead of you, and you have said, why can't I go, too?

> But the Lord says...no, because I am causing you to be a horse trained in battle, a horse of warfare, and when I let you go, I will ride on you in power. And when I say go this way, you will go this way, and when I restrain you, you will be restrained. Had I released you beforehand, you would have run ahead of me into disaster. The Lord said I am going to train you to walk by faith and not by sight, and you will perform great accomplishments because of the faith I have established in you.

Her words broke something off me. I felt an oppression lift.

I went to her after the meeting and asked her what I needed to do to participate with the word. She said to trust the Lord because he is trustworthy, and he will make a way for me, even if there seems to be no way.

She encouraged me to love; to forgive those who had hurt or offended me; to pray in the Spirit to build up my faith; to ask the Lord to help my unbelief; and to remember that my strength is not by might or power but by the Spirit of the Lord.

I followed her counsel.

Driving through South Africa's desert areas for hours at a time on my job, I prayed in the Spirit and sought the Lord. And I discovered that he was there with me and, strangely enough, he wanted to speak to me.

Gradually, I came to a place where I had peace, and in that peace, my faith exploded. I was able to hear and believe phenomenal things and obey the Holy Spirit, no matter how crazy it sounded.

Everything in God's Kingdom, especially prophecy, arises out of and is contingent upon faith. Faith is the alpha and omega of prophecy, just as it is the prerequisite for salvation and the spiritual gifts.

"[W]ithout faith," Scripture declares unequivocally, "it is impossible to please God, because anyone who comes to him must believe that he exists and that he rewards those who earnestly seek him."[25]

It is not *nearly* impossible or really quite difficult to please God without faith. It is impossible. No options. No short cuts. No exceptions.

By extension, without faith, it is impossible to prophesy. Contrariwise, *with* faith, anything—and everything—is possible, through the Holy Spirit.

By faith, Joshua commanded the sun to stand still.

> So the sun stood still, and the moon stopped, until the nation avenged themselves of their enemies. Is it not written in the book of Jashar? And the sun stopped in the middle of the sky and did not hasten to go down for about a whole day.[26]

By faith, Israel passed through the Red Sea as on dry land.

> [B]ut when the Egyptians tried to do so, they

---

[25] Hebrews 11:6.
[26] Joshua 10:12-13 NASB.

12

were drowned.[27]

By faith, the walls of Jericho fell after the people had marched around them for seven days.[28]

> And what more shall I say? I do not have time to tell about Gideon, Barak, Samson and Jephthah, about David and Samuel and the prophets, who through faith conquered kingdoms, administered justice, and gained what was promised; who shut the mouths of lions, quenched the fury of the flames, and escaped the edge of the sword; whose weakness was turned to strength, and who became powerful in battle and routed foreign armies. Women received back their dead, raised to life again.[29]

So just what is faith?

The biblical definition is that "faith is the *substance* of things hoped for, the *evidence* of things not seen."[30] But what does that mean? How can anything we can't see have substance? How can it be evidence?

Noah Webster defined *substance* as "that which really is or exists; equally applicable to matter or spirit. Thus the soul of man is called an immaterial substance, a cogitative substance, a substance endued with thought."

He defined *evidence* as "that which elucidates [makes clear] and enables the mind to see truth."[31]

Therefore, even though it is imperceptible to our senses, faith is an immaterial substance that enables our mind to see the truth, the essence and embodiment of which is Jesus Christ.[32]

---

[27] Hebrews 11:29.
[28] Hebrews 11:30.
[29] Hebrews 11:32-35.
[30] Hebrews 11:1 NKJV, emphasis added.
[31] Webster, Noah, *American Dictionary of the English Language*, 1828, Vol. II, p.84.
[32] John 14:6.

When Peter discerned the true identity of Jesus, declaring him to be "the Messiah, the Son of the living God," Jesus replied, "Blessed are you, Simon son of Jonah, for this was not revealed to you by flesh and blood, but by my Father in heaven."[33] Peter believed by faith, which is not only irrefutable proof but also the source of unlimited power.

> "Truly I tell you, if you have faith as small as a mustard seed, you can say to this mountain, 'Move from here to there,' and it will move. Nothing will be impossible for you."[34]

Though faith cannot be weighed on our scales or measured by our standards, it is quantifiable. It can increase or decrease. Praying in tongues increases our faith.

> Anyone who speaks in a tongue edifies themselves.[35]

Unbelief diminishes it.

> "Where did this man get this wisdom and these miraculous powers?" they asked. "Isn't this the carpenter's son? Isn't his mother's name Mary, and aren't his brothers James, Joseph, Simon and Judas? Aren't all his sisters with us? Where then did this man get all these things?"

> And they took offense at him.

> But Jesus said to them, "A prophet is not without honor except in his own town and in his own home."

> And he did not do many miracles there because of their lack of faith.[36]

---

[33] Matthew 16:16-17.
[34] Matthew 17:20.
[35] 1 Corinthians 14:4.
[36] Matthew 13:54-58.

Faith is a gift, and we all start out with just enough to say yes to Jesus. From that point on, it costs us to increase our faith.

> Consider it nothing but joy, my brothers and sisters, whenever you fall into various trials. Be assured that the testing of your faith [through experience] produces endurance [leading to spiritual maturity, and inner peace]. And let endurance have its perfect result *and* do a thorough work, so that you may be perfect and completely developed [in your faith], lacking in nothing.[37]

Every trial is an opportunity to grow in faith.

There are essentially two kinds of faith. Faith is given to us when we are born again. And there is extraordinary faith that is a gift of the Spirit.[38]

Faith is creative.

> "*Let* there be light!"

> "*Let* the land produce vegetation!"

> "*Let* us make man in our image, in our likeness!"[39]

Let! Let! Let! Who or what was God talking to?

> Now the earth was formless and empty, darkness was over the surface of the deep...[40]

He was talking to Formlessness, Emptiness, and Darkness, commanding them to conform to his will.

By the power of faith, we are able to speak to the circumstances in

---

[37] James 1:2-4 AMP.
[38] 1 Corinthians 12:9.
[39] Genesis 1, emphasis added.
[40] Genesis 1:2.

our life that contradict God's prophetic will for us and command them to conform to his will. We are able to speak to the mountains in our life and remove them by the same power that raised Jesus Christ from the dead.

Faith can be sacrificial.

Sometimes, I just have to lay on the altar what I love most and trust the Lord to provide a ram in the thicket.

> By faith Abraham, when God tested him, offered Isaac as a sacrifice. He who had embraced the promises was about to sacrifice his one and only son, even though God had said to him, "It is through Isaac that your offspring will be reckoned." Abraham reasoned that God could even raise the dead, and so in a manner of speaking he did receive Isaac back from death.[41]

The Lord used sacrificial faith to break the hold of adrenalin over my life. Because of all the violence in my home, in school, and in the military, I became addicted to adrenalin rushes.

South Africa's famous Table Mountain looms 3,500 feet above Cape Town. Every Saturday morning, I used to climb it along with ex-military buddies from my church. It was a great adrenalin high. The air was fresh and clear and we could see for miles. It made us feel closer to God somehow.

One morning, about five o'clock, we met as usual, geared up and ready to go. I took point and we headed up the rock face to meet with God. On a ledge part way up, the Holy Spirit dropped a thought into my head.

When I asked him what it meant, he told me we were going to be disappointed if we expected to meet him on top of the mountain. He said there was strife between my friends and their wives. So I turned to them and asked which one had had an argument with his wife last

---

[41] Hebrews 11:17-19.

16

night or this morning. They all acknowledged that they were in disagreement with their wives over one issue or another.

I told them I was going back down and home to my wife, and it was fine with me if they went on by themselves. When they asked why, I told them the Lord had impressed upon me that climbing the mountain to find him was a waste of time.

They looked astonished but shrugged it off and continued their climb.

At home, the Holy Spirit showed me in his Word why my prayers were being hindered and ineffective. For one thing, God had set me apart for a special relationship with him and my associations were blocking it.

Can two walk together, unless they are agreed?[42]

For another, I needed to change my relationship with my wife. In South African culture, wives are not held in very high esteem. In God's kingdom, marriage is held to a much higher standard.

In the same way, you husbands, live with *your wives* in an understanding way [with great gentleness and tact, and with an intelligent regard for the marriage relationship], as with someone physically weaker, since she is a woman.

Show her honor *and* respect as a fellow heir of the grace of life, so that your prayers will not be hindered *or* ineffective.[43]

I had also been trying to build an intimate relationship with God on a foundation of highs, like Christians who pursue spiritual sensations through an endless chain of conferences and mountaintop experiences. The paradox is that the greatest changes and our most intimate encounters with the Holy Spirit occur in the valleys and deserts of our lives.

---

[42] Amos 3:3 NKJV.
[43] 1 Peter 3:7 AMP.

17

Faith is transformational.

We are transformed by faith from victims to overcomers as we are enabled more and more to see things, circumstances, and people from God's perspective. We are not on earth looking up to heaven, separated from him by mesosphere, troposphere, and stratosphere. We are seated with Christ in heavenly places,[44] and from that vantage point we see the world differently. Transforming faith enables us to reckon ourselves inside God's kingdom, looking out at the world rather than inside the world, peering into the kingdom of God. It helps us be transformed from orphans into children and heirs.

Faith pleases God.

If it is impossible to please God without faith, the converse is also true, that we please him by exercising our faith—aggressively looking beyond flesh and circumstances in order to gaze into his eyes, perceive his reality, get close enough for a hug and a kiss.

> ...anyone who comes to him must believe that he exists and that *he rewards those who earnestly seek him.*[45]

The reward of faith is deeper intimacy with, and revelation of, God. The Song of Solomon offers a moving picture of pleasing faith.

> "Turn your eyes from me," the King says to the Shulamite girl. "They overwhelm me."[46]

While this book is viewed by many as a collection of love poems between a lover and his beloved, others see it as an allegory of the intimacy between Jesus and his bride, the church.

That God can be "overwhelmed" is in itself an overwhelming idea, but also a wonderfully tender one and a notion that is entirely in keeping with his nature and character.

---

[44] Ephesians 2:6-7.
[45] Hebrews 11:6, emphasis added.
[46] Song of Songs 6:5.

The eyes, philosophers tell us, are the windows to the soul, and the soul is the source of our thoughts, will, and emotions.

This image, then, is of God gazing into the eyes of his church, his bride, and seeing that every thought, her entire will, and all her emotions are for him. And the sight is so beautiful to him that he asks her to look away, just for a moment, while he catches his breath.

In the movie *Chariots of Fire*, Eric Liddell says, "God made me fast. And when I run, I feel His pleasure."[47]

Nothing is more rewarding than delighting God.

Faith empowers us to respond to warnings that may make no sense to the natural man.

> By faith Noah, when warned about things not yet seen, in holy fear built an ark to save his family. By his faith he condemned the world and became heir of the righteousness that is in keeping with faith.[48]

A warning might be a simple feeling or a gentle nudge. God's prophets need to develop a listening lifestyle, like a surfer sitting on his board out where the waves break. His feet dangle in the water, waiting to feel that slight change in the undercurrent that tells him to paddle for all he's worth if he wants to ride, rather than be sucked under, the approaching wave.

Driving to a church one night where I was going to minister, I prayed for the Holy Spirit to be with me and guide me. I began to feel uneasy, as if he was warning me, so I kept praying.

I stopped for a red light at a very busy intersection. But when the light changed, I hesitated about forty seconds, as the guy behind me honked impatiently for me to go.

---

[47] According to the Eric Liddell Center in Edinburgh, Scotland, Eric Liddell never actually said this. It was written for the film by screenwriter Colin Welland, but it illustrates the point. Retrieved 06-11-16 from http://www.ericliddell.org/ericliddell/quotations.
[48] Hebrews 11:7.

Just as the car on the opposite side started through the intersection, I looked to my left and saw an 18-wheeler, headlights off, and he wasn't slowing down. He barreled right through the red light, narrowly missing the oncoming car.

I cannot tell you how grateful I was that I had been forewarned. Even the horn-blowing driver behind me waved a thank you to me for waiting. In addition to saving my life, that experience boosted my faith and enabled me to minister with even greater impact that night in the assurance that the Holy Spirit was with me.

Faith enables us to obey.

> By faith Abraham, when called to go to a place he would later receive as his inheritance, obeyed and went, even though he did not know where he was going.[49]

After my pastor prophesied that God "will take you to the nation where I spoke to your heart at the gateway," the Holy Spirit began to confirm his word through multiple witnesses. Recalling my experience in 1976 at the Statue of Liberty, the "gateway" to America, I knew my destination was the United States. But America is a big country. So I inquired of the Lord. Where specifically do I go? Who do I need to help me? What do I need to do?

I never heard any clear word, but a friend assured me, "If you knock, he will open!"

So I wrote letters to the governors of three states where I thought I would like to live. Texas Governor Ann Richards was the only one to reply. She sent me all the information I needed and even had two members of the U.S. Consulate (who happened to be Texans) come to my home to see if there was anything else I needed to move to the Lone Star State.

The Holy Spirit instructed me to take no contact information of people I could call in the States to help me out. There was to be no

---

[49] Hebrews 11:8.

"safety net." He would guide me day by day.

It was cold and overcast when we arrived at Dallas/Ft. Worth International Airport. No one was waiting for us, and we had no idea of where to go next. But God used a skycap[50] to get us a hotel room where his brother worked. That was our first step into the unknown, but it was far from our last.

Every day, the Holy Spirit led us to new places, new people. Each day was an adventure, a step of faith, like Indiana Jones stepping off the cliff's ledge, trusting that a bridge would be under his foot, despite the fact that all he could see was the bottom of the canyon thousands of feet below.[51] And over the years, my nervous uncertainty has developed into a calm trust that, like his peace, is beyond my understanding.

Faith transcends circumstances and even death. It is faith in God's promises, despite evidence to the contrary, that remains solid even if we don't live to see them fulfilled.

> All these people were still living by faith when they died. They did not receive the things promised; they only saw them and welcomed them from a distance, admitting that they were foreigners and strangers on earth.[52]

Faith is life-giving. We have the power of life, regardless of the fact that death dwells in our mortal bodies.

> And by faith even Sarah, who was past childbearing age, was enabled to bear children because she considered him faithful who had made the promise.[53]

Faith empowers us to align our soul with our spirit, until the realities

---

[50] Airport porter.
[51] *Indiana Jones and the Last Crusade* (1989), Lucasfilm Ltd., starring Harrison Ford, Sean Connery, and Alison Doody
[52] Hebrews 11:13.
[53] Hebrews 11:11.

of God's kingdom become more real than our perceptions of the world. It is not becoming "so heavenly minded that we're no earthly good;" it is becoming so heavenly minded that we're on the same page with the Holy Spirit.

The enemy scoffs and says this is impossible; God smiles and says this is normal Christianity.

I called out a young couple once, and as they came up, I heard the pitter-patter of baby feet and baby laughter. I thought, how cute, but I held off saying anything.

I told them God understood that their journey had been a sad one, and I prophesied about the plan the Lord had for them. They broke down and cried, and the Spirit of the Lord prompted me to pray against premature death that had plagued their home.

The wife told me they had been married twelve years and had tried many methods to conceive, including multiple surgeries, but there was no breakthrough. The doctor told them conception was impossible, due to the endometriosis that blocked her fallopian tubes.

The Holy Spirit directed me to pray over their reproductive ability, break them free from barrenness, and take authority over the doctor's prognosis. He revealed to me that they had suffered six miscarriages and that, by the end of the year, they would conceive and deliver a healthy baby girl. I shared this with them and told them about the pitter-patter and laughter.

The wife said her sister had the same problem and had suffered four early-term miscarriages. About two months later, I received an email from the husband, thanking me for the prayer and announcing that they had just learned they were pregnant.

The next time I ministered at their church, I was blessed to be able to hold their baby daughter. And as if that wasn't enough, I also held her sister's baby boy, conceived at the same time as his cousin!

The Lord holds the keys to life, and he determines the outcome.

Conceptual faith enables us to believe and trust him until we see it come to pass or die trusting.

Faith, in short, is the enabler of the prophetic.

CHAPTER TWO
the astounding, formidable Holy Spirit

Late have I loved you, O Beauty ever ancient, ever new, late
have I loved you! You were within me, but I was outside,
and it was there that I searched for you. In my unloveliness
I plunged into the lovely things which you created. You
were with me, but I was not with you. Created things kept
me from you; yet if they had not been in you they would
have not been at all. You called, you shouted, and you broke
through my deafness. You flashed, you shone, and you
dispelled my blindness. You breathed your fragrance on me;
I drew in breath and now I pant for you. I have tasted you,
now I hunger and thirst for more. You touched me, and I
burned for your peace.[54]

~ Augustine of Hippo

Prophecy is all about Jesus, the Christ.

The Holy Spirit—wholly God and the presence and power of
Jesus in his people on earth—is the all-in-all of the prophetic.

Prophecy is not just about foretelling the future; it is an intimate
interaction between the prophet and the Holy Spirit to prepare and/or
equip one, many, or all of God's people for a subsequent interaction
with the Holy Spirit.

The prophet's principle ministry is to stand before the Lord,
ministering to the Lord by sacrificing his time and attention—his
most precious and irreplaceable commodities—to God. The public
face of the prophet's ministry is merely the fruit of his private
ministry to the Lord. It is the power and love of Christ in him
affecting those around him, the glory of God that clings to him,[55] the

---

[54] Augustine of Hippo, *Confessions*, Book X, Chapter 27, circa 400 A.D., Penguin Classics;
New Impression edition, 1961.
[55] Exodus 34:29-35.

virtue of God that goes forth from him, as when the woman with the issue of blood touched Jesus[56] or when Peter's shadow fell on the ill and infirm.[57] It is the evidence that he has been with Jesus.[58]

Prophecy is not about impressing people with the godliness of the prophet; prophetic words are a continuing revelation of Jesus Christ and his kingdom.

When I was about seven years old, I spent a school holiday with my Aunty Sheila, one of my father's youngest sisters. I had been taken to her home to heal after a severe beating by my father.

Aunty Sheila had experienced a face-to-face encounter with Jesus and was the most spiritual of my aunties. I remember her praying over dinner and reading Scripture and talking about heaven. I was fascinated that there could be a place where there was no pain. At this stage in my life, I had experienced a lot of pain, and the comfort of her love and voice always made me feel good.

She made me *melkkos*,[59] my favorite food. I always thought about that place called heaven when I was eating melkkos, because she would talk about how there would be no crying in heaven. We would sit on her big bed, all my cousins and I, and listen to her talk about her encounter with Jesus, and she would tell us stories from the Bible. It was a great place of healing for me.

One day, she called me aside and said that my life had been ordered by the Lord, that he had put a great gift in me and, despite the hardships I had endured, he loved me and would guide me, and I would play a great role one day in his purpose for his church. When I left after the holiday, I forgot what she said because life continued to be a struggle for me. I even forgot the taste of melkkos.

After I was saved by the Lord in 1985, I went to visit her to tell her that the Jesus she had spoken to me about had come to find me. She

---

[56] Luke 8:43-48.
[57] Acts 5:12-16.
[58] Acts 4:1-13.
[59] *Melkkos* is a South African staple, a cooked concoction of boiled milk, flour, and cinnamon sugar.

hugged me and wept and told me how many times she had prayed for me while I was in the military, that the Lord would preserve me from being killed. And she reminded him of the word she had declared over me as a little boy. I was preserved by the Spirit of prophecy.

I had forgotten this story until I started to write this book and the Holy Spirit reminded me.

After I left South Africa to come to America, I never saw my Aunty Sheila again. She was violently murdered in 2011. I was at Los Angeles International Airport, heading to Australia when I heard the news of her death.

I was broken and angry and wanted to change my flight to South Africa to find the men who had violated and murdered her. Sitting in the departure lounge, I wept and asked the Lord how such a kind, beautiful person's life could end so horribly. She loved everyone and never hurt anyone.

The Lord spoke to me clearly and said, "Vengeance is mine." He said my Auntie Sheila had been martyred and was with him in glory and that I should continue my course here on earth.

Like my relationship with my auntie, the Holy Bible—the foreshadow and fulfillment of the redemption of God's creation through the death, burial, and resurrection of his Son—begins and ends with prophecy.

In Genesis, Moses, God's first prophet, records the awesome account of the creation of the universe as it was personally revealed to him by the Creator.

Scripture concludes with the prophesies of John, which the apostle declares to be "the revelation of Jesus Christ." Just before the end of the Bible, John defines the spirit of prophecy. And even that is wrapped in a glorious cloud of revelation of God's Son.

> Hallelujah! Salvation and glory and power belong
> to our God, because His judgments are true and

righteous; for He has judged the great harlot who was corrupting the earth with her immorality, and He has avenged the blood of His bondservants on her.... Hallelujah!... For *the testimony of Jesus is the spirit of prophecy.*[60]

Prophecy is an expression of the power and love of Jesus through the special gifts imparted to God's people by the Holy Spirit.

The last recorded words of Jesus before he ascended into heaven to return to his Father are a promise of power and prophecy:

I am going to send you what my Father has promised; but stay in the city until you have been clothed with power from on high.[61]

While the life and teaching of Jesus are the heart of prophecy, the Holy Spirit is its power. The two are inseparable, just as the Trinity is indivisible.

One of Judaism's most sacred Scriptures is known as the *sh'ma.*

Sh'ma Yisrael Adonai Eloheinu Adonai Eḥad.
Hear, O Israel, the LORD our God, the LORD is one.[62]

The Hebrew word *ehad* is more clearly translated "a unity." In the beginning, God said, "Let *Us* make man in *Our* image, according to *Our* likeness."[63]

God is a unity, yet a plurality, similar to man who is a unity, yet a plurality of body, soul, and spirit that struggle with one another for dominance.

So I find this law at work: Although I want to do good, evil is right there with me. For in my inner

---

[60] Revelation 19:1, 4, 10 NASB, emphasis added.
[61] Luke 24:49.
[62] Deuteronomy 6:4.
[63] Genesis 1:26 NASB.

being I delight in God's law; but I see another law at work in me, waging war against the law of my mind and making me a prisoner of the law of sin at work within me.[64]

As each part of man functions independently, yet interdependently, so too each person of the Godhead functions uniquely, yet interdependently, and in perfect harmony and agreement.

Our Father draws us into his kingdom.

No one can come to Me unless the Father who sent Me draws him; and I will raise him up on the last day.[65]

Jesus holds everything together.

And He Himself existed *and* is before all things, and in Him all things hold together. [His is the controlling, cohesive force of the universe.][66]

The Holy Spirit empowers us to live supernatural lives.

Let me put this question to you: How did your new life begin? Was it by working your heads off to please God? Or was it by responding to God's Message to you? Are you going to continue this craziness? For only crazy people would think they could complete by their own efforts what was begun by God. If you weren't smart enough or strong enough to begin it, how do you suppose you could perfect it? Did you go through this whole painful learning process for nothing? It is not yet a total loss, but it certainly will be if you keep this up! Answer this question: Does the God who lavishly provides you with his own presence,

---

[64] Romans 7: 21-23.
[65] John 6:44 NASB.
[66] Colossians 1:17 AMP.

his Holy Spirit, working things in your lives you could never do for yourselves, does he do these things because of your strenuous moral striving *or* because you trust him to do them in you?[67]

But just who is this amazing member of the Godhead?

We don't much relate to the Holy Spirit as a person. More often, Christians relate to the Holy Spirit the way a Jedi relates to The Force. If I talk about worshiping the Holy Spirit, it almost sounds cultish. Yes, he is one of the persons of the Trinity. Yes, he is fully God. But he just doesn't seem huggable, like Jesus. We can't see ourselves climbing onto his lap as we do with our Father. And many of us just can't seem to get the picture of that Luke 3:22 dove out of our heads—especially Christians here in Texas where dove season is one of the premier events of the year.[68]

One Sunday, a Dallas pastor set a stuffed dove on the pulpit and began his sermon by declaring, "The Holy Spirit is not a bird!" That might sound funny, and it got a laugh from the congregation. But it was also a sobering moment, as many realized they had indeed been thinking of the Holy Spirit as an "it" and picturing him as a sort of a divine peace symbol.

While it is true that, "As soon as Jesus was baptized…heaven was opened, and he saw the Spirit of God descending like a dove and alighting on him," there are many other things that are vital for us to understand about this person of the Godhead.

I was like a sponge after I was saved, soaking up everything I could

---

[67] Galatians 3:2-6 MSG.

[68] Valdez, Andrea, "How to Hunt Dove," *Texas Monthly* magazine, September 2009: "To many hunters, Labor Day weekend is synonymous with the soft coos of the mourning dove. Every year, roughly 350,000 people in Texas are seduced by this avian siren song and harvest about five million of the four-ounce birds—that's about 30 percent of the total number shot in the U.S. Why is dove hunting so popular here? 'Texas has more dove than any other state,' says Corey Mason, who oversees the game bird program for the Texas Parks and Wildlife Department. 'It's an inexpensive, social sport that can be enjoyed by almost everyone.' Before you dust off your 12-gauge, note some favorable new regulations: The statewide daily bag limit has been upped to fifteen birds, and the north and central zones now enjoy longer, seventy-day seasons." Retrieved June 19, 2016 from http://www.texasmonthly.com/the-culture/how-to-dove-hunt.

about God. But the Holy Spirit had me stumped. I heard people say you need to tarry to receive him, whatever that meant. Some said you need to be clean and obedient. Others countered that you don't need the Holy Spirit at all, you just need Jesus. There were even people who said speaking in tongues was from the devil. I thought about that and told them I had served the devil for thirty-four years and never once spoke in tongues—I swore a lot but, no sir, never spoke in tongues.

The more I heard, the more intrigued I became with the function and purpose of the Holy Spirit. When I talked to my mentor and to my pastor, both said it was an absolute necessity to be baptized and filled with the Holy Spirit in order to be directed by the Spirit and receive revelation of Jesus.

As I studied the Bible and read everything it said about the Holy Spirit, my desire to know and experience him became more intense. Every day, I prayed and asked for intimacy and filling of the Holy Spirit. But the greater my desire to know him grew, the more my mind and flesh opposed me. *You're already saved*, my mind said. *You've done what is required to go to heaven.*

But I couldn't shake the deep hunger to know him. I prayed even more for the baptism of the Holy Spirit. I read the Word many times a day. I was like someone obsessed. This was back when I was traveling all the time in the pharmaceutical business.

One day, as I was driving along, begging the Lord to know him better and to learn my purpose in life, there was a *whoosh!* and the next minute I felt like I was on fire! I was speaking in some strange language. I couldn't contain myself. I was afraid and wept uncontrollably. I didn't know what to do.

Was this the Holy Spirit?

I pulled over to the side of the road, got out, dropped to my knees in the desert sand, and began to thank the Father. I don't know why, but I shouted like I never had before. Something had broken off me, and I was flying free, my spirit was soaring, my mind was flooded, my body felt electrified.

"Speak, Lord," I said, "I am listening."

I heard a verse from Scripture: "Lord, you know all things; you know I love you."

Then I heard the voice of Jesus say to me, "Feed my sheep."[69]

Since that day I have been driven by a passion to reveal the Lord to his people and to the world. And the Holy Spirit has remained close, teaching me more about Jesus and his kingdom and revealing through me what he wants to share with those to whom he sends me.

It's hard to describe the irrational comfort I feel whenever I am truly outside my comfort zone and out of my depth. Sometimes I feel incredibly insecure about my abilities and overwhelmed by the opportunities he sends my way. Then I pray in the Spirit, the prophetic words flow, and my shadowy doubts and anxieties disappear in his light. I feel I can climb any mountain. The little prompts and gentle nudges say "go here," "do this," "say this," "don't be afraid; I am with you even unto the end." Sometimes I feel him all around me and the hair on the back of my neck stands up as if the air is alive with static electricity.

Since that day in the desert, he has remained with me, no matter what. And as my intimacy with the Lord continues to grow, the guidance and prompting of the Holy Spirit becomes more clear and understandable.

Every relationship between a believer and the Holy Spirit, however, is unique. Mine is not yours; yours is not your cousin Amy's.

Comparing ourselves with one another leads to discontent and unbelief. It leaves us vulnerable to spiritual abuse, that is, to being persuaded by others, the devil, or even ourselves that we don't measure up because we don't see or experience the things of God the way someone else does.

For example, people experience the baptism of the Spirit in lots of

---

[69] John 21:17.

different ways. One is not more valid or effective than another, for there is one Holy Spirit and he empowers each of us as he chooses.[70]

The question is not what should we experience, but just who is the Holy Spirit?

If we begin with that question, we will find the correct answer. Unfortunately, we often begin by asking *"What* is the Holy Spirit?" which makes him impersonal, does him great injustice, and leads us off in the wrong direction.

For one thing, the Holy Spirit is the evidence that the kingdom of God has come to earth, manifest through the gifts he gives to men.

> And with great power the apostles were giving testimony to the resurrection of the Lord Jesus, and abundant grace was upon them all.[71]

The Holy Spirit is one with the Father and the Son. Like the Father and the Son, he is eternal and omnipotent. It was the Holy Spirit who empowered Christ to offer himself to God, unblemished, as a living sacrifice to atone fully and in perfect righteousness for the sins of mankind.[72]

The Holy Spirit is omnipresent—pervasive, existing everywhere in all things at all times.

> Where can I go from your Spirit? Where can I flee from your presence?[73]

He is omniscient, the only true Know-It-All.

> What no eye has seen, what no ear has heard, and what no human mind has conceived—the things God has prepared for those who love him—these are the things God has revealed to us by his Spirit.

---

[70] 1 Corinthians 12:11.
[71] Acts 4:33 NASB.
[72] Hebrews 9:14.
[73] Psalm 139:7.

The Spirit searches all things, even the deep things of God.[74]

Like us, the Holy Spirit has emotions.

> Don't cause the Holy Spirit sorrow by the way you live. Remember, he is the one who marks you to be present on that day when salvation from sin will be complete.[75]

We can learn more about him by meditating on his many names.

For example, he is the Spirit of Truth.

> But when he, the Spirit of truth, comes, he will guide you into all the truth. He will not speak on his own; he will speak only what he hears, and he will tell you what is yet to come. [76]

He is the Spirit of Holiness.

> Paul, a servant of Christ Jesus, called to be an apostle and set apart for the gospel of God—the gospel he promised beforehand through his prophets in the Holy Scriptures regarding his Son, who as to his earthly life was a descendant of David, and who through the Spirit of holiness was appointed the Son of God in power by his resurrection from the dead: Jesus Christ our Lord.[77]

He is the Spirit of Life

> Therefore, there is now no condemnation for those who are in Christ Jesus, because through Christ Jesus the law of the Spirit who gives life

---

[74] 1 Corinthians 2:9-10.
[75] Ephesians 4:30 TLB.
[76] John 16:13.
[77] Romans 1:1-4.

33

has set you free from the law of sin and death. [78]

He is the Spirit of Glory.

> If you are insulted because of the name of Christ,
> you are blessed, for the Spirit of glory and of God
> rests on you. [79]

He is our champion and teacher.

> But the Advocate, the Holy Spirit, whom the
> Father will send in my name, will teach you all
> things and will remind you of everything I have
> said to you. [80]

He is the Spirit of Adoption and Sonship.

> The Spirit you received does not make you slaves,
> so that you live in fear again; rather, the Spirit you
> received brought about your adoption to sonship.
> And by him we cry, *"Abba,* Father." [81]

He is the Spirit of Judgment and Fire

> The Lord will wash away the filth of the women
> of Zion; he will cleanse the bloodstains from
> Jerusalem by a spirit of judgment and a spirit of
> fire. [82]

And he is a River of Living Water.

> "Whoever believes in me, as Scripture has said,
> rivers of living water will flow from within them."
> By this he meant the Spirit, whom those who
> believed in him were later to receive. Up to that

---

[78] Romans 8:1-2.
[79] 1 Peter 4:14.
[80] John 14:26.
[81] Romans 8:15.
[82] Isaiah 4:4.

time the Spirit had not been given, since Jesus had not yet been glorified.[83]

Since Pentecost, the Holy Spirit has been at work in the individual believer, in the church, and in the world. He is not someone who drops in from time to time, just on Sundays, or in small group meetings. He's not summoned, conveniently within reach, or on the distant end of a prayer. The Holy Spirit lives in us 24-7-365. We're his base of operations. We're where he keeps his stuff, where he's comfortable, where he's free to kick back and be himself. He's with us when we're doing well in our own eyes and when even we can't stand to hang out with us.

> Do you not know that your bodies are temples of the Holy Spirit, who is in you, whom you have received from God?[84]

The Holy Spirit gives us dynamic supernatural gifts. And he knows every believer so intimately that he gives us the precise gift we need, as much as we need, the exact moment we need it, for as long as we need it.

> There are different kinds of gifts, but the same Spirit distributes them. There are different kinds of service, but the same Lord. There are different kinds of working, but in all of them and in everyone it is the same God at work....
>
> All these are the work of one and the same Spirit, and *he distributes them to each one, just as he determines.*[85]

When we need to intercede in prayer for a person, situation, group, or even a nation, but have no knowledge of circumstances or the Father's will, "the Holy Spirit prays for us with such feeling that it cannot be expressed in words."[86]

---

[83] John 7:38-39.
[84] 1 Corinthians 6:19.
[85] 1 Corinthians 12:4-6, 11, emphasis added.
[86] Romans 8:26 TLB.

In short, he is our Everything. He is the presence of Jesus after Jesus returned to the Father.

> "If you [really] love Me, you will keep *and* obey My commandments. And I will ask the Father, and He will give you another Helper (Comforter, Advocate, Intercessor—Counselor, Strengthener, Standby), to be with you forever—the Spirit of Truth, whom the world cannot receive [and take to its heart] because it does not see Him or know Him, *but* you know Him because He (the Holy Spirit) remains with you *continually* and will be in you.[87]

In addition to his intimate relationship with the individual believer, the Holy Spirit is the glory and power of Christ in the church corporately. He is the entryway for the individual believer into the body of Christ on earth and the force that holds the church together.

> For by one [Holy] Spirit we were all baptized into one body, [spiritually transformed—united together] whether Jews or Greeks (Gentiles), slaves or free, and we were all made to drink of one [Holy] Spirit [since the same Holy Spirit fills each life].[88]

The Holy Spirit is the architect of the church.

> What a foundation you stand on now: the apostles and the prophets; and the cornerstone of the building is Jesus Christ himself! We who believe are carefully joined together with Christ as parts of a beautiful, constantly growing temple for God.

> And you also are joined with him and with each other by the Spirit and are part of this dwelling place of God.[89]

---

[87] John 14:15-17 AMP.
[88] 1 Corinthians 12:13 AMP.
[89] Ephesians 2:20-22, TLB.

Aided by the prophets, the apostles are the builders. As the foundation, the apostles and prophets also bear the weight of the structure. Jesus is the cornerstone, the first stone set. He determines the position of every other element in the structure. He is the reference for every other stone.

The Holy Spirit is the manifestation of the Godhead.

> The Holy Spirit displays God's power through each of us as a means of helping the entire church. To one person the Spirit gives the ability to give wise advice; someone else may be especially good at studying and teaching, and this is his gift from the same Spirit. He gives special faith to another, and to someone else the power to heal the sick. He gives power for doing miracles to some, and to others power to prophesy and preach. He gives someone else the power to know whether evil spirits are speaking through those who claim to be giving God's messages—or whether it is really the Spirit of God who is speaking. Still another person is able to speak in languages he never learned; and others, who do not know the language either, are given power to understand what he is saying.
>
> It is the same and only Holy Spirit who gives all these gifts and powers, deciding which each one of us should have.[90]

Above all, he glorifies Jesus.

> He shall praise me and bring me great honor by showing you my glory.[91]

Finally, the Holy Spirit is active not only in the individual believer and in the church but also in our fallen world, convicting the world of sin and offering sinners forgiveness, reconciliation, and eternal

---

[90] 1 Corinthians 12:7-11 TLB.
[91] John 16:14 TLB.

life with the Father.

> Unless I go away, the Advocate will not come to
> you; but if I go, I will send him to you. When he
> comes, he will prove the world to be in the wrong
> about sin and righteousness and judgment: about
> sin, because people do not believe in me; about
> righteousness, because I am going to the Father,
> where you can see me no longer; and about
> judgment, because the prince of this world now
> stands condemned.[92]

The Holy Spirit is a giver. He gives glory to God, structure to the
church, hope to the world, and power to the believer.

And what power!

---

[92] John 16:7-11.

CHAPTER THREE
gifts of the Spirit

> Will God ever ask you to do something you are not able to do? The answer is yes—all the time! It *must* be that way, for God's glory and kingdom. If we function according to our ability alone, we get the glory; if we function according to the power of the Spirit within us, God gets the glory. He wants to reveal *Himself* to a watching world.[93]
>
> ~ Henry T. Blackaby

G od gives.

In the beginning, he exhaled his essence into a dust-man, transforming this new creation into his own image and likeness. Thousands of years later, God gave his only Son to pay the penalty for the sins of mankind.

> For God was pleased to have all his fullness dwell in him, and through him to reconcile to himself all things, whether things on earth or things in heaven, by making peace through his blood, shed on the cross.[94]

And after Jesus was raised from the dead and returned to his Father, God gave the Holy Spirit to about 120 of his disciples.

A tornadic roar shook the room. Heavenly fire appeared and separated into blazing tongues that settled on each of them but which, like Moses' bush,[95] neither burned nor consumed.

---

[93] Blackaby, Henry T., *Experiencing the Spirit: The Power of Pentecost Every Day*, Multnomah, 2009, p. 7, italics his, ISBN: 978-1-59052-911-9.
[94] Colossians 1:19-20.
[95] Exodus 3.

Then, as suddenly as it had begun, the noise stopped. And with their ears still ringing, the disciples heard themselves babbling. But it wasn't babble. Nor was it Hebrew or Greek or Aramaic. It was weird. And weird draws crowds. People from a score of nations pressed in around the disciples as they boldly declared the Son of God and his kingdom. Everybody heard the stunning news in his own language. It was like the UN without interpreters. Most were amazed and wanted to know more. About 3,000 received Jesus as their Messiah, and "the Lord added to their number daily those who were being saved."[96]

Once, as I was praying with a pastor for a woman, he began to pray in tongues, repeating the same phrase about a dozen times.

"*Baphume USanthane!*" he commanded again and again, having no clue what he was saying. But as a South African, I recognized the Zulu words. They meant, "Come out, Satan!" Had the Holy Spirit prompted him to speak in his own language, he might have hesitated or resisted.

As he repeated these words, the woman was thrown to the ground and delivered from whatever had been ailing her.

When she got up, she looked like a new person, and the Holy Spirit gave me a word for her about how the Lord had set her free from depression and a suicidal spirit. She confirmed that she had been in and out of a psychiatric facility and had cut her wrists twice during the past few months.

But tongues is only one of the many gifts imparted by the Holy Spirit, all of which are a huge deal!

While love is important above all things, because God *is* love,[97] the gifts of the Spirit arguably run a tight second.

Pursue love, yet desire earnestly spiritual gifts...[98]

---

[96] Acts 2:41, 47.
[97] 1 John 4:8.
[98] 1 Corinthians 14:1 NASB.

40

When we exercise the gifts of the Holy Spirit, we transcend the laws of nature and glorify God.

Jesus knew we could never, in our own strength and wisdom, fulfill our mandate to "go and make disciples of all nations, baptizing them in the name of the Father and of the Son and of the Holy Spirit, and teaching them to obey everything I have commanded you."[99] We would succeed only by the power of the Holy Spirit, because "the kingdom of God is not a matter of talk but of power.[100]

So what exactly are these powerful supernatural gifts? Scripture mentions nine of them: three dynamic gifts, three discerning gifts, and three declarative gifts.

dynamic gifts – the power to do

The *gift of faith* differs from ordinary, everyday faith in that it is *extra*ordinary faith for a specific and limited situation or purpose. Think faith on steroids or spiritual adrenalin.

One night, after tossing and turning for hours, I got up and went to my office to pray. I put on some soft worship music to help quiet my thoughts. After reading the Word and praying a while, I sensed the Lord nudging me to take a step of faith.

I had saved $600 toward a new laptop, and I felt the Holy Spirit prompt me to withdraw it in the morning. I understood the money was to be seed, but I didn't know when and where to plant it.

I made the withdrawal and waited all day but heard nothing more. That night I went to bed early, hoping to catch up on lost sleep, but the same thing happened. About four o'clock, I gave up trying to sleep and went to my office. As I prayed, I had a sense that the Lord wanted me to get in my car and drive to a particular location. I arrived, parked, and waited.

Three hours later, a man carrying a suitcase walked up to the bus stop across the street, and the Lord prompted me to go over and talk

---

[99] Matthew 28:19-20.
[100] 1 Corinthians 4:20.

to him. He looked tired and worn. I asked where he was going, and he said his mother was dying and he was traveling by bus from Arizona to Louisiana to be with her. While changing buses in Dallas, two men had robbed him of his wallet and ticket. I asked how much he needed to complete his trip, and he said $400. I reached into my pocket and gave him the $600. I explained how the Lord had brought me to him, and he told me he had worked hard to raise the money for the bus ticket and was trusting the Lord for a miracle.

O Lord, how manifold are Your works![101]

The Holy Spirit imparted the gift of faith to two men to bring them together at a bus stop—one with a problem, the other with the Lord's provision.

This illustrates another vital lesson for the emerging prophet: prayer is our default. Prayer, not prophecy, is the language of the prophet. Prayer—not confusion, complacency, or anxiety—should be our response whenever and however the Holy Spirit interrupts our work, recreation, ministry, or sleep.

Like Samuel, when he was awakened by the Lord, the prophet's response needs to be "Speak LORD, for your servant is listening."[102]

It's also a good to develop the habit of allowing God to finish his sentences. When the Holy Spirit told me to withdraw the money, he obviously wasn't finished. What was I supposed to do with it? So I waited to hear more. When he directed me to a particular location, he still wasn't finished. Why am I here? And despite voices swirling around my head for three hours saying *You missed God* or *You can go home now, God was just testing your obedience,* or *God just wanted to know if you would give him control of your money,* it was clear to me that he wasn't finished yet, because he hadn't spoken again. So I waited as long as it took to allow the Spirit to finish what he had to say.

You may be wondering whether God pulled a new laptop out of a hat for me. Unfortunately, most testimonies about giving these days

---

[101] Psalm 104:24 NKJV.
[102] 1 Samuel 3:9.

seems to end with getting, under the banner of God's faithfulness. But we obey, not because we're guaranteed to get or even because God is faithful. We obey—circumstances, experience, and reason notwithstanding—because he is God.

The *gift of healing* is the power to cure, to make whole. Like the other gifts of the Spirit, it declares and demonstrates that the kingdom of God is here. This gift is about supernatural healing, healing that defies medical explanation. It is not an anomaly, the healing power of hope, or the psychological power of a placebo.

At the beginning of our ministry, back in 1994, I prayed for a young couple at a church in Arizona. I've prayed for thousands of people since then and rarely remember what the Lord said to them. But I remember this one because it didn't end that night. It's a glorious illustration of the power and affection of the Holy Spirit. But this is Linda Killian's story,[103] and I want her to tell it:

> "Our lives were quite a mess when we met Ron Campbell. Just a few months earlier, my husband Larry had been diagnosed with terminal Mesothelioma cancer. And if that wasn't enough to deal with, our youngest son Brian was suffering with severe OCD (Obsessive Compulsive Disorder). The voice inside him never allowed him to sit to eat, he had to eat everything before taking even a sip of water, he had to fill the tub and then empty it before he could take a shower, touch all the corners of the pillows on the bed fifty times, touch all the door knobs, count to a certain number before passing through a doorway, and on and on. OCD is the ultimate manifestation of salvation by works, ruled with an iron fist by the Spirit of Fear.
>
> "I had prayed for my husband for twenty years to truly give his life to Christ, but he lived the way he wanted, and we suffered at times because of it.

---

[103] Reprinted by permission. See also Brian's book, *OCD, The Way Out*, Xlibris, 2010 at Amazon.com, ASIN: B003FGWUYK.

"I knew God would deliver my husband and bring him into a true relationship with him, and he did...right before the cancer was diagnosed.

"By the time Brian was twenty-one, the OCD was so disabling that he couldn't hold a job. And now my husband was told to go home and get his affairs in order. He was given a year to eighteen months to live.

"When I was a young woman, God had healed me of Lupus and a blood clot in my leg. I knew what he could do. I went to what I knew, to the place of power on my knees. I prayed, and I waited.

"One day, a friend told me she had gone to a church home group and heard a prophet from South Africa. I had never heard of a modern-day prophet, but she said he told her things that only she and God knew and shared how it had changed her. A week later, she called to say that this prophet, named Ron Campbell, was going to be ministering at a church in Arizona, in the same city where our eldest son and his new bride lived. I called them and told them about the meeting, never really expecting them to go. But they did.

"'Mom, Dad,' they said afterward, 'we went to that church you told us about and this man called us up front.'

"Then, over the phone, they played a recording of the words he spoke over them. As Larry and I listened, we were overwhelmed with joy.

"Meanwhile, the cancer continued to drain my husband's life, and Brian sank deeper into the isolation of OCD.

"During those days, a group of women came to

my home on Wednesdays to pray. I called Brian and asked if I could share about his OCD and have them pray for him, assuring him that it would stay within the group. At first he said it was nobody's business, but finally he allowed me to tell them.

"A couple days later, the friend who had told me about Ron Campbell said she had shared about Brian with her husband, who then contacted Ron.

Ron called them back to say that he couldn't get Brian off his mind and asked if he could get together and pray for him.

"While my heart jumped for joy, I realized that I would have to tell Brian that someone had talked about him outside the group. Would he be mad at me? Would I lose all relationship with him?

But I realized that fear was from the enemy, not the Lord. So, when he came home from lunch, I just dove in and said it all.

"I'll never forget the look of anger on his face as I started to tell the story, but by the end of it, he broke and the tears flowed.

"'Mom,' he said, 'something's got to happen because I can't live like this much longer.' I didn't know it then, but Brian had been planning to commit suicide.

"Two weeks later, Brian called to tell me that the meeting was set for that Saturday. He didn't want Larry or me to be there, and that was fine with us. We just wanted him healed. We told him to come back to the house after prayer, and at that moment Larry and I began to intercede.

"In two hours, we heard his truck pull in. The door

slammed, and we called out that we were in the backyard. I'll always remember the smile on our son's face as he walked through that gate. I had not seen him smile in years. And when this six-foot-five kid reached us, he grabbed us and hugged us with the best bear hug ever. That too was special because we had not been allowed to touch him for more than a year, because he was told by the voice that we would die if we did.

"We couldn't stop laughing and crying. We made our way into the house, asking him to tell us all about what this prophet had said and done.

"'First,' he said, 'look where I'm sitting!'

"He was on the sofa, a place where the demonic voice had not allowed him to sit in seven years, forcing him always to sit on the floor!

"He said this man from South Africa had told him to stand up and raise his hands. Then he began to break strongholds—the spirits of death, fear, Freemasonry, and racism.

"'Who is Dean?' Ron had asked suddenly.

"Brian told him Dean was a friend he had in New Jersey when he was in the eighth grade. That was when the OCD started.

"'I break the power of witchcraft and occultism that entered with this relationship in the name of Jesus.' Ron said.

"Brian then told him how he and Dean had played with the Ouija board and asked spirits to come.

"'We did even worse things,' he told us, 'but Ron broke them all, and I'm free!'

46

"So Ron Campbell, a man we had still never met, had prayed for both our boys, and we were seeing this dramatic change in each. I knew in my spirit that my husband had to be next.

"Four weeks later, Larry and I were at someone's home because we had heard that Ron was going to minister there.

After he prayed for two couples, he looked at me and my husband and asked if he could pray for us.

"The words of healing were beyond anything we could have ever comprehended. We knew Larry was healed that night.

"My husband had already been given five chemotherapy treatments, and we had just received the CT scan report that Friday that said there was no change in the six-inch tumor.

"Another chemotherapy treatment was scheduled for Monday. Before the treatment began, Larry told the doctor that he had been healed over the weekend and that no more chemo would be needed.

"The doctor was furious. We asked for another scan, but the doctor said Larry wasn't due for one for another three months.

"In the word Ron had given us, the Holy Spirit had said, 'Right now you are battling, but in three months, you will see a totally different picture.' The Lord already knew what the doctor was going say, and he was letting us know, 'I've got this.'

"The wait was difficult. The enemy tried to convince us that Larry would be consumed by cancer before the time was up and we would look like fools. But we held on, and when the next CT scan report came, it showed nothing."

The third dynamic gift is the *working of miracles*, an extraordinary virtue to instantly do something supernatural.

When a woman who had suffered an issue of blood for twelve years touched Jesus' clothes, she was instantly healed of that plague, and Jesus knew "in himself that virtue had gone out of him."[104] After his friend Lazarus died and was decomposing in the tomb, Jesus called out to him, and "the dead man came out, his hands and feet wrapped with strips of linen, and a cloth around his face."[105]

> Jesus did many other things as well. If every one of them were written down, I suppose that even the whole world would not have room for the books that would be written.[106]

Yet, he made us an amazing promise:

> Very truly I tell you, whoever believes in me will do the works I have been doing, and they will do even greater things than these, because I am going to the Father.[107]

discerning gifts – the power to reveal

A *word of knowledge* is possessing facts you could know only by the revelation of the Holy Spirit. Jesus received a word of knowledge when he met Philip's brother.

> Jesus saw Nathanael coming toward Him, and said of him, "Behold, an Israelite indeed, in whom is no deceit."

> Nathanael said to Him, "How do You know me?"

---

[104] Mark 5:30 KJV.
[105] John 11:44.
[106] John 21:25.
[107] John 14:12.

Jesus answered and said to him, "Before Philip called you, when you were under the fig tree, I saw you."

Nathanael answered and said to Him, "Rabbi, You are the Son of God! You are the King of Israel!"

Jesus answered and said to him, "Because I said to you, 'I saw you under the fig tree,' do you believe? You will see greater things than these."[108]

When the early church was established, all the believers shared their possessions with one another...all except a couple named Ananias and Sapphira. They sold some property and pretended to give the money to the community so they would look good. But some of it stuck to their pockets.

With his wife's full knowledge he kept back part of the money for himself, but brought the rest and put it at the apostles' feet.[109]

The Holy Spirit gave Peter a word of knowledge.

"What made you think of doing such a thing?" Peter asked the surprised Ananias. "You have not lied just to human beings but to God." Ananias dropped dead, "and great fear seized all who heard what had happened."[110]

I was flying back to Dallas one day after ministering at a church in Atlanta, tired and eager to get home. But I felt uneasy about this particular flight, which was very unusual, and the closer we got to boarding, the more uneasy I felt.

I prayed and delayed boarding to wait for wisdom from the Holy Spirit. He told me the flight was overbooked and they would soon

---

[108] John 1:47-50 NKJV.
[109] Acts 5:2.
[110] Acts 5:1-5.

ask for passengers who would give up their seats and take a later flight. When they did, he said, I should volunteer my seat.

Then the announcement came. They asked for five volunteers and promised to boost us up to business class on a flight leaving a couple of hours later and give us a $400 voucher in addition. I plowed my way to the gate and gave the agent my boarding pass.

I had no idea why the Holy Spirit hadn't wanted me on that flight. It taxied out and took off without incident, so I walked to my new gate, settled in, and relaxed.

About twenty-five minutes later, there was a flurry of activity. Emergency vehicles raced toward the runway. A plane was in distress, and a hush fell over the people on the concourse.

I still didn't put two and two together.

We watched as the plane attempted to land. Sparks flew and fire trucks drove into the smoke as the plane finally slowed to a stop with all the emergency exits opened and slides deployed.

When I finally boarded my new flight, some of the passengers from the damaged plane were aboard. They said the cabin had filled with smoke after taking off and they didn't expect to survive. It was a miracle, they said, that they all made it.

A *word of wisdom* differs from a word of knowledge. Wisdom is "the right use or exercise of knowledge, the choice of laudable ends, and of the best means to accomplish them."[111]

> The fear of the LORD is the beginning of wisdom, and knowledge of the Holy One is understanding.[112]

Jesus frequently astounded the chief priest and Pharisees with words of wisdom. Even as a boy, his wisdom confounded them. After he disappeared during the Passover festival, his parents "found him in

---

[111] Webster, Vol. II p.113.
[112] Proverbs 9:10.

the temple courts, sitting among the teachers, listening to them and asking them questions. Everyone who heard him was amazed at his understanding and his answers."[113] Then there was the time the Pharisees tried to entrap Jesus.

> "Teacher," they said, "we know that you are a man of integrity and that you teach the way of God in accordance with the truth. You aren't swayed by others, because you pay no attention to who they are. Tell us then, what is your opinion? Is it right to pay the imperial tax to Caesar or not?"
>
> But Jesus, knowing their evil intent, said, "You hypocrites, why are you trying to trap me? Show me the coin used for paying the tax."
>
> They brought him a denarius, and he asked them, "Whose image is this? And whose inscription?"
>
> "Caesar's," they replied.
>
> Then he said to them, "So give back to Caesar what is Caesar's, and to God what is God's."
>
> When they heard this, they were amazed. So they left him and went away.[114]

Words of knowledge and wisdom are the most familiar and visible gifts today in the prophetic and tend to define and validate the prophetic. But being prophetic—even more prophetic than a prophet—does not make one a prophet. It is not a substitute for the prophetic call, anointing, and authority. People are titillated when a prophet "reads their mail," tells them something specific like their birthdate, phone number, address, or the names of family members. This is all of the Lord, but there is far more to the prophetic.

I was invited to minister at a church once, along with two other people who functioned in the prophetic. As the meetings progressed,

---

[113] Luke 2:46-47.
[114] Matthew 22:16-22.

however, it turned into a "battle of the prophets," each displaying his ability to hear the Lord and manifest his gift more specifically than the last one. It was impressive, and the congregation started looking for and expecting more and more glitter and gleam.

My time had not come yet, but I had been watching and listening. Back in my hotel room, I fasted and prayed and begged the Holy Spirit for even more accuracy, more details than my predecessors. Looking back, I wonder whether the fasting wasn't more of a hunger strike to try to coerce the Holy Spirit into pushing down a bit harder on the accelerator.

While I prayed, the Lord dropped a thought into my spirit.

"Why?" That was all.

"I need to make an impact," I replied.

Yuck! The feeling hit me the moment the words were out of my mouth. I couldn't believe I had been sucked in to playing Can You Top This?[115]

Then the Lord spoke something surprising to my spirit.

"Receiving the word of wisdom or the word of knowledge does not make you a prophet. I have called you to be my prophet. Now be content. If you function in your office, you will have power and authority to transform hearts and lives."

Striving is always a warning sign. Supernatural gifts are presents from the Holy Spirit. He gives them as he chooses, when he chooses, to whom he chooses in whatever measure he chooses. The moment we step out of his will and begin to do anything supernatural, we have stepped from ministry into sorcery and witchcraft. We have walked away from the Holy Spirit into the arms of the devil.

When we exercise *discernment of spirits*, the Holy Spirit exposes to us the spirit, or spirits, operating in a person or situation.

---

[115] Radio panel game (1940-1954) in which comedians tried to top one another's jokes, as determined by a "laugh meter."

Someone may seem to exhibit a gift of the Holy Spirit, for example, but actually be practicing sorcery, like the slave girl who followed Paul around Philippi.

> Once when we were going to the place of prayer, we were met by a female slave who had a spirit by which she predicted the future. She earned a great deal of money for her owners by fortune-telling…. Finally Paul became so annoyed that he turned around and said to the spirit, "In the name of Jesus Christ I command you to come out of her!" At that moment the spirit left her.[116]

The discernment of spirits came in handy when we first arrived in America. As I said, we had no idea where the Lord wanted us to live. So I began to pray and ask him to give me direction and bring me into the right relationships.

One day, driving down a highway in Fort Worth, the Holy Spirit gave me a word of knowledge. He told me to drive to a specific address and ask to talk to a man named Jason.[117] When I arrived, his secretary told me he was booked for the day and would not be able to see me.

I excused myself, went to the restroom, and asked the Lord if I had heard him clearly. He told me to proceed, so I went back. Jason's secretary told me her boss's lunch appointment was a no-show and his calendar was clear. He would see me. I asked the Lord why I was here, and he said "to gain wisdom."

Jason was very well dressed and impeccably groomed, in contrast to my T-shirt, jeans, and flip flops. I shared with him why I had come to the U.S. and how the Holy Spirit had given me his name and address and sent me to speak to him. As I talked, he sat in a big leather rocker, seemingly ignoring me. I could see a spirit of religion all over him, judging me. Suddenly, Jason stood abruptly and stalked out of his office. He returned about five minutes later,

---

[116] Acts 16:16, 18.
[117] I've used a different name to protect his privacy.

handed me a business card, and told me to call the person on the card.

"Next time you come to me for help," he said as I left, "make sure you dress accordingly. Otherwise, I will not see you!" I thanked him for his help and left wiser than when I had arrived. The Holy Spirit had taught me that an important ability in finding the right relationships is recognizing the wrong ones.

declarative gifts – the power to create

The *gift of tongues* is the ability to speak in a language unknown to us. It may be a language of men or of angels.[118] And Scripture says it should be standard equipment for all believers.

> And these signs will follow those who believe: In My name they will cast out demons; they will speak with new tongues.[119]

Tongues is the only gift that was manifest in the upper room at Pentecost.

> All of them were filled with the Holy Spirit and began to speak in other tongues as the Spirit enabled them.[120]

It was also the first gift manifested in public, a gift so powerful that it jump-started the church and launched the expansion of the kingdom of God.

> Now there were staying in Jerusalem God-fearing Jews from every nation under heaven. When they heard this sound, a crowd came together in bewilderment, because each one heard their own language being spoken. Utterly amazed, they asked: "Aren't all these who are speaking Galileans? Then how is it that each of us hears them in our native

---

[118] 1 Corinthians 13:1.
[119] Mark 16:17.
[120] Acts 2:4.

language? Parthians, Medes and Elamites; residents of Mesopotamia, Judea and Cappadocia, Pontus and Asia, Phrygia and Pamphylia, Egypt and the parts of Libya near Cyrene; visitors from Rome (both Jews and converts to Judaism); Cretans and Arabs—we hear them declaring the wonders of God in our own tongues!" Amazed and perplexed, they asked one another, "What does this mean?...

Those who accepted his message were baptized, and about three thousand were added to their number that day.[121]

Tongues is a multi-purpose gift. Paul explained to the church in Corinth that the gift of tongues is a sign for unbelievers,[122] referring to the previous verse in which God spoke through Isaiah about rebellious Israel.

With men of other tongues and other lips I will speak to this people; and yet, for all that, they will not hear Me.[123]

In other words, God spoke to Israel through his prophets in a language they understood. When, like unbelievers, they ignored him, he "spoke" to (chastised) them through their enemies, who spoke a foreign language.

The gift of tongues also strengthens the believer. He who speaks in tongues edifies (builds up, fortifies, enlightens) himself.[124] In addition, tongues strengthens and deepens our fellowship with the Holy Spirit.

For he who speaks in a tongue does not speak to men but to God, for no one understands him; however, in the spirit he speaks mysteries.[125]

---

[121] Ibid., 5-12, 41.
[122] 1 Corinthians 14:22.
[123] Ibid. v.21 NKJV.
[124] 1 Corinthians 14:4.
[125] 1 Corinthians 14:2 NKJV.

An interesting dynamic of prayer is that it builds both soulish and spiritual bonds. When we pray for our enemies, for example, we may find ourselves imperceptibly developing an affection for them, which cracks open the door to reconciliation. When we pray with one another, we grow in affection for one another, which strengthens marriages. At the same time, when we pray *in* the Spirit, we pray *with* the Spirit, deepening our affection for him and providing opportunities for him to share God's secrets with us.

Tongues guarantees that we pray according to God's will.

> Likewise the Spirit also helps in our weaknesses. For we do not know what we should pray for as we ought, but the Spirit Himself makes intercession for us with groanings which cannot be uttered. Now He who searches the hearts knows what the mind of the Spirit is, because He makes intercession for the saints according to the will of God.[126]

And the Holy Spirit worships through us when we pray in tongues.

> But the hour is coming, and now is, when the true worshipers will worship the Father in spirit and truth; for the Father is seeking such to worship Him. God is spirit, and those who worship Him must worship in spirit and truth.[127]

For the gift of tongues to be of even more value to believers, the Holy Spirit gifted us with the *interpretation of tongues*, through which he reveals the meaning of the unintelligible language so that we can translate with understanding.

> What then shall we say, brothers and sisters? When you come together, each of you has a hymn, or a word of instruction, a revelation, a tongue or an interpretation. Everything must be done so that the church may be built up. If anyone speaks in a

---

[126] Romans 8:26-27 NKJV.
[127] John 4:23-24 NKJV.

tongue, two—or at the most three—should speak, one at a time, and someone must interpret. [128]

The sixth spiritual gift is *prophecy*, speaking the mind of God under divine unction. This gift is singled out among all the rest.

> Pursue love, and desire spiritual gifts, *but especially that you may prophesy*. For he who speaks in a tongue does not speak to men but to God, for no one understands him; however, in the spirit he speaks mysteries. But he who prophesies speaks edification and exhortation and comfort to men.

> He who speaks in a tongue edifies himself, but he who prophesies edifies the church. I wish you all spoke with tongues, *but even more that you prophesied*; for he who prophesies is greater than he who speaks with tongues, unless indeed he interprets, that the church may receive edification.. [129]

Prophecy is a six-fold gift of the Holy Spirit. It is given for edification, exhortation, and comfort, as well as confirmation, learning, and building faith. Edification means to build up. When the disciples asked Jesus what signs to look for at the end of the age, Jesus warned that there would be persecution. At the same time, he built them up.

> But when they arrest you and deliver you up, do not worry beforehand, or premeditate what you will speak. But whatever is given you in that hour, speak that; for it is not you who speak, but the Holy Spirit. [130]

In the same way, Paul edified the church in Thessalonica. He warned them that "the man of lawlessness...will oppose and will exalt

---

[128] 1 Corinthians 14:26-27.
[129] 1 Corinthians 14:1-5 NKJV, emphasis added.
[130] Mark 13:11 NKJV.

himself over everything that is called God or is worshiped, so that he sets himself up in God's temple, proclaiming himself to be God." At the same time, he encouraged the saints by adding, "but the one who now holds it back will continue to do so till he is taken out of the way. And then the lawless one will be revealed, whom the Lord Jesus will overthrow with the breath of his mouth and destroy by the splendor of his coming."[131]

Prophecy exhorts. It inspires other believers, as Paul exhorted Timothy.

> Do not neglect your gift, which was given you through prophecy when the body of elders laid their hands on you. Be diligent in these matters; give yourself wholly to them, so that everyone may see your progress. Watch your life and doctrine closely. Persevere in them, because if you do, you will save both yourself and your hearers.[132]

Prophecy comforts us in tribulation.

> I know your afflictions and your poverty—yet you are rich! I know the slander of those who say they are Jews and are not, but are a synagogue of Satan. Do not be afraid of what you are about to suffer. I tell you, the devil will put some of you in prison to test you, and you will suffer persecution for ten days. Be faithful, even to the point of death, and I will give you life as your victor's crown.[133]

Prophecy confirms a believer's spiritual destiny.

> When Jesus came to the region of Caesarea Philippi, he asked his disciples, "Who do people say the Son of Man is?"

---

[131] 2 Thessalonians 2:3-4; 7-8.
[132] 1 Timothy 4:14-16.
[133] Revelation 2:9-10.

They replied, "Some say John the Baptist; others say Elijah; and still others, Jeremiah or one of the prophets."

"But what about you?" he asked. "Who do you say I am?" Simon Peter answered, "You are the Messiah, the Son of the living God."

Jesus replied, "Blessed are you, Simon son of Jonah, for this was not revealed to you by flesh and blood, but by my Father in heaven. And I tell you that you are Peter, and on this rock I will build my church, and the gates of Hades will not overcome it. I will give you the keys of the kingdom of heaven; whatever you bind on earth will be bound in heaven, and whatever you loose on earth will be loosed in heaven."[134]

Prophecy educates the believer in his destiny.

Preach the Word; be prepared in season and out of season; correct, rebuke and encourage—with great patience and careful instruction. For the time will come when men will not put up with sound doctrine. Instead, to suit their own desires, they will gather around them a great number of teachers to say what their itching ears want to hear. They will turn their ears away from the truth and turn aside to myths.

But you, keep your head in all situations, endure hardship, do the work of an evangelist, discharge all the duties of your ministry.[135]

Finally, prophecy builds faith, establishing it in the believer.

See what great love the Father has lavished on us, that we should be called children of God! And that

---

[134] Matthew 16:13-19.
[135] 2 Timothy 4:2-5.

is what we are! The reason the world does not know us is that it did not know him. Dear friends, now we are children of God, and what we will be has not yet been made known. But we know that when Christ appears, we shall be like him, for we shall see him as he is. All who have this hope in him purify themselves, just as he is pure.[136]

Remember that the Holy Spirit "distributes [his gifts] to each one, just as he determines."[137] All of the gifts do not manifest all the time in every person. He gives to *whom* he will *when* he will.

It took more than a dozen years to finalize our citizenship after Melanie and I immigrated to America. Because of my background, our application was preceded by seemingly endless interviews and stringent background checks by Interpol, the FBI, and other agencies, plus the usual inoculations and medical screenings. One particular interview had me worried about whether we would be allowed to remain in the US.

We had changed our visa classification and somebody had questions. I spent all morning praying, then sat in the waiting room pleading with the Lord for a kind inspector.

Suddenly, I heard my name called and turned to see the meanest, angriest-looking person I could imagine. My stomach knotted. I couldn't sense the presence of the Lord at all.

We sat silently in her office as she pored over my file. I continued to pray, reaching blindly into heaven, trying to touch God's hand. Then a word came to me.

"Who is Tomas?" I asked her. She said it was her brother. I took her hand and began to prophesy over her.

"Your brother is in a hospital. He is dying of an incurable disease, and the person who abused him also abused you." She trembled and cried as I continued to declare the word of the Lord over her. I told

---

[136] 1 John 3:1-3.
[137] 1 Corinthians 12:11.

her the Lord had sent me to her to break the shame and guilt and that he was going to heal her brother.

She sank down behind her desk, still holding my hand and sobbing. I released her hand and awaited my fate.

When she had composed herself, she stamped the papers "Approved," then came over and hugged me. Her countenance had changed completely.

Though I didn't feel God's presence or have a prophetic word when I walked into that office, the Spirit anointed me with his declarative power at just the right moment to disarm the situation, liberate the inspector, heal her brother, and give me favor with the authorities.

godly character

In addition to giving gifts, the Holy Spirit grows fruit. Fruit is all about character.

> "Watch out for false prophets. They come to you in sheep's clothing, but inwardly they are ferocious wolves. *By their fruit you will recognize them.* Do people pick grapes from thornbushes, or figs from thistles? Likewise, every good tree bears good fruit, but a bad tree bears bad fruit. A good tree cannot bear bad fruit, and a bad tree cannot bear good fruit. Every tree that does not bear good fruit is cut down and thrown into the fire. Thus, *by their fruit you will recognize them.*"[138]

Other translations say they are "ravening" wolves, meaning hungry and hunting for prey. They are plotters and deceivers, always and intentionally seeking victims. The natural tendency of the carnal man is to recognize a person's calling by his gifting. If someone prophesies, he is a prophet. But God says our fruit, not our gift, reveals or exposes who we truly are. A prophet is false, not because

---

[138] Matthew 7:15-20, emphasis added.

his words are false but because his life is false.

> The acts [fruit] of the flesh are obvious: sexual immorality, impurity and debauchery; idolatry and witchcraft; hatred, discord, jealousy, fits of rage, selfish ambition, dissensions, factions and envy; drunkenness, orgies, and the like. I warn you, as I did before, that those who live like this will not inherit the kingdom of God. But the fruit of the Spirit is *love, joy, peace, forbearance, kindness, goodness, faithfulness, gentleness and self-control.* Against such things there is no law. Those who belong to Christ Jesus have crucified the flesh with its passions and desires. Since we live by the Spirit, let us keep in step with the Spirit.[139]

We need to keep in mind that performing miracles and casting out demons are not fruit of the Spirit. Jesus warned that false prophets will point to these acts as proof that they are God's ministers. But, he said, they are lawless and don't even know him.[140]

As we exercise the gifts of the Holy Spirit, interacting with him and deepening our intimacy with him, there should be evidence that his fruit is growing in us.

> If I speak in the tongues of men and of angels, but do not have love, I am only a resounding gong or a clanging cymbal. If I have the gift of prophecy and can fathom all mysteries and all knowledge, and I have a faith that can move mountains, but do not have love, I am nothing.[141]

But doesn't the Lord say we're not supposed to judge one another?

> Do not judge, or you too will be judged. For in the same way you judge others, you will be judged, and

---

[139] Galatians 5:19-25, bracket and emphasis added.
[140] Matthew 7:22-23.
[141] 1 Corinthians 13:1-2.

with the measure you use, it will be measured to you.[142]

We are not judging one another; we are recognizing fruit.

Some people believe a leader's personal life doesn't matter. What really matters, they say, is how well the pastor, politician, or corporate executive does the job. Once again, God says otherwise.

> An elder must be blameless, faithful to his wife, a man whose children believe and are not open to the charge of being wild and disobedient. Since an overseer manages God's household, he must be blameless—not overbearing, not quick-tempered, not given to drunkenness, not violent, not pursuing dishonest gain. Rather, he must be hospitable, one who loves what is good, who is self-controlled, upright, holy and disciplined. He must hold firmly to the trustworthy message as it has been taught, so that he can encourage others by sound doctrine and refute those who oppose it.[143]

And Paul asks rhetorically, "if anyone does not know how to manage his own family, how can he take care of God's church[144]" or a corporation, city, state, or nation? How much more must the prophet, who represents God and speaks his thoughts, grow the fruit of love, patience, and self-control!

When I was new in the Lord and had received many words about being called as a prophet, I developed an attitude of self-importance. I felt comfortable when people were afraid of me, since that seemed how biblical prophets commanded respect. I believed that, when you delivered the word, it had to be booming and full of the fire of the Lord. I justified being unkind to people by telling myself this was just the prophetic nature. I wasn't aware at the time that it was nothing but arrogance and impatience. But that would soon change.

---

[142] Matthew 7:1-2.
[143] Titus 1:6-9.
[144] 1 Timothy 3:5.

One day, a prophetic voice came to our church and said the Lord had called me to be a prophet to the nations. It was wild! After the meeting, our pastor asked me to come to his office to talk about all the wonderful things I was experiencing. When I arrived, we had a cup of tea and exchanged the usual pleasantries. Then he asked me for a favor.

"Sure," I said, "anything." I was excited. I thought, *here we go, all these prophetic words...this is my moment to shine.*

I would indeed shine, but not in the way I expected.

"I need someone to clean the restrooms before Sunday morning service," he said. Our church met in a movie theater, and the restrooms could get pretty nasty by the weekend.

I didn't know whether to be outraged or just offended.

"Didn't you hear that I am called as a prophet to the nations? How can you ask me to shine sinks and clean toilets? Don't you know who I am?"

"You can begin your ministry in the toilet," he said, "or you can end it there. Your choice."

Next Sunday morning, I scrubbed and washed and flushed and sprayed the toilets and sinks, military style.

As you may have noticed, our pastor was direct and blunt. He was also intense. And when his preaching got a little too hot, the men would filter into the restroom for a breather. That Sunday, however, they ended up jumping from the pan into the fire.

There is a reason why many places of business post signs in the men's rooms telling guys to wash up. Cleanliness is not necessarily part of the male DNA. But no signs were needed in our loo that morning. It had an angry prophet.

"Hey, man, wash your hands!...Dry your hands!...Whoa, clean up your mess!"

"…and come here and let me pray for you!"

When I wasn't barking at them, I prophesied over them, and some were delivered.

The Holy Spirit turned the men's room into a place of ministry and brought peace and resolution to the lives of a number of men. He also planted seeds in me which would, in his time and by his grace, yield fruit.

CHAPTER FOUR
prophetic genealogy

If a church is built with the ministry of the apostle alone, without the prophet ministry, it may become so doctrinally structured and ordered that it becomes lifeless and formal without the fiery flow of praise and power. If it is built by the prophet alone, without the ministry of the apostle, the people may become so spiritually activated that everyone is a law unto himself or herself, and it could lead to fanaticism. But with the ministry of both the apostle and prophet the Church of Jesus Christ will maintain a balance between structure and spirituality, doctrine and demonstration, prophetic perspective and apostolic order.[145]

~ Dr. Bill Hamon

The prophetic path began thousands of years ago with Moses and the men the Holy Spirit anointed to build the Tabernacle.

Then the LORD said to Moses, "See, I have chosen Bezalel son of Uri, the son of Hur, of the tribe of Judah, and I have filled him with the Spirit of God, with wisdom, with understanding, with knowledge and with all kinds of skills—to make artistic designs for work in gold, silver and bronze, to cut and set stones, to work in wood, and to engage in all kinds of crafts.

Moreover, I have appointed Oholiab son of Ahisamak, of the tribe of Dan, to help him."[146]

---

[145] Hamon, Bill, *Apostles, Prophets and the Coming Moves of God: God's End-Time Plans for His Church and Planet Earth*, Destiny Image Publishers, Inc., 1997, pp. 175-176, ISBN: 0-939868-09-1.
[146] Exodus 31:1-6.

An apostle is loosely defined as "a person deputed to execute some important business."[147] Merrill F. Unger's Bible dictionary adds that "it seems to have been preeminently that of founding the churches, and upholding them by supernatural power specially bestowed for that purpose."[148]

Bezalel was a type of apostle, deputed by God to build his Tabernacle and supernaturally inspired and empowered to design and execute virtually every kind of required art and craft.

Bezalel means "in the shadow (protection) of God." Israel's twelve tribes encamped on the four sides of the Tabernacle. In its shadow, protected by God's presence, the Israelites were safe and secure.

The work of an apostle is to design, build, and oversee, to purge sin and preach redemption. The apostle recognizes, installs, and disciples leaders and helps people find their place and function in the body of Christ.

Bezalel created designs and blueprints. He also worked with gold, which symbolizes glory and kingship.

> On coming to the house, they saw the child with his mother Mary, and they bowed down and worshiped him. Then they opened their treasures and presented him with gifts of gold, frankincense and myrrh.[149]

Silver symbolizes redemption.

> The first offspring of every womb, both man and animal, that is offered to the LORD is ours.

> But you must redeem every firstborn son and every firstborn male of unclean animals. When they are a month old, you must redeem them at the redemption price set at five shekels of

---

[147] Webster, Vol. I, p.11.
[148] Unger, Merrill F., *Unger's Bible Dictionary*, Moody Press, Chicago, 1957, p.73.
[149] Matthew 2:11.

silver, according to the sanctuary shekel, which weighs twenty gerahs.[150]

"You were not redeemed with perishable things like silver or gold from your futile way of life inherited from your forefathers," Peter explained, 'but with precious blood, as of a lamb unblemished and spotless, the blood of Christ."[151]

Bronze symbolizes sin. When Daniel interpreted Nebuchadnezzar's dream,[152] he said the belly and thighs of the statue were bronze that will rule over the whole earth. The bronze kingdom of Persia indeed ruled over the whole earth under the influence of the demonic prince that ruled Persia.[153]

Cut and set stone symbolizes living stones.

> And coming to Him as to a living stone which has been rejected by men, but is choice and precious in the sight of God, you also, as living stones, are being built up as a spiritual house for a holy priesthood, to offer up spiritual sacrifices acceptable to God through Jesus Christ.[154]

Work in wood speaks of leaders. City gates were often made of reinforced wood and served as a meeting place for leaders.

> The gate was the place for great assemblies of the people, as they passed into and out of the city.

> This naturally led to the custom of using gates as places for public deliberation; reading the law and proclamations; holding court; gathering news and gossip; attracting the attention of the sovereign or dignitary at his going out or coming in. The priests and prophets seem to have delivered their

---

[150] Numbers 18:15-16.
[151] 1 Peter 1:18-19 NASB.
[152] Daniel 2:39.
[153] Daniel 10:12-13.
[154] 1 Peter 2:4-5 NASB.

discourses, admonitions, and prophecies at the gates.[155]

The apostle, like the church, is reflected in the Tabernacle—humble before God's glory, champion of God's redemption, fierce enemy of sin, protector of God's people, and father to God's leaders.

Oholiab, on the other hand, was a type of prophet. *Oholiab* means "father's tent." The prophet Moses dwelled in the "tent of his Father."

> Now Moses used to take a tent and pitch it outside the camp some distance away, calling it the "tent of meeting." Anyone inquiring of the LORD would go to the tent of meeting outside the camp. And whenever Moses went out to the tent, all the people rose and stood at the entrances to their tents, watching Moses until he entered the tent.
>
> As Moses went into the tent, the pillar of cloud would come down and stay at the entrance, while the LORD spoke with Moses. Whenever the people saw the pillar of cloud standing at the entrance to the tent, they all stood and worshiped, each at the entrance to their tent. The LORD would speak to Moses face to face, as one speaks to a friend.[156]

Oholiab was of the tribe of Dan, which means "Judge." Judges defended and administrated Israel between the death of Joshua and the coronation of Saul.

> Now Deborah, *a prophet*, the wife of Lappidoth, was leading Israel at that time. She held court under the Palm of Deborah between Ramah and Bethel in the hill country of Ephraim, and the Israelites went up to her to have their disputes decided.[157]

---

[155] Unger, p. 392.
[156] Exodus 33:7-11.
[157] Judges 4:4-5, emphasis added.

Even the standard of the Tribe of Dan speaks to the prophetic genealogy of Oholiab. Upon a red and white field was the crest of an eagle, the iconic seer and foe to serpents. An eagle's eye is like a telephoto lens that can spot the smallest mouse a hundred feet below. It sees not only colors but also ultraviolet light that enables it to spot traces of bodily fluid left by prey. And with eyes angled thirty degrees from the midline, it has a 340-degree field of vision.[158]

Ever since Bezalel and Oholiab co-labored to build and equip the Tabernacle of the Lord, apostles and prophets have worked together to build his kingdom.

Somewhere along the line, however, theologians decided that apostles and prophets no longer exist or are no longer needed. Unger, for example, declares that:

> [The apostolic office] ceased…with its first holders, all continuation of it, from the very conditions of its existence being impossible. The bishops of the ancient Churches coexisted with, and did not in any sense succeed, the apostles…[159]

And according to the Christian Research Institute:

> Clearly many men today who claim to be apostles have taken upon themselves authority over other people which has not been given to them by God.

> Additionally, they are making prophetic utterances which they falsely claim to be divinely inspired.[160]

But if there are no apostles and prophets today, there can be no pastors, teachers, or evangelists.[161] God's word is all or nothing. It

---

[158] "How does human vision compare to that of an eagle?", The Visionary Blog, Lasik MD, Canada's Lasik provider, retrieved 05-18-16 from http://www.lasikmd.com/blog/how-does-human-vision-compare-to-that-of-an-eagle.
[159] Unger, p. 73.
[160] "Are there apostles and prophets today?" Christian Research Institute, retrieved 05-18-16 from http://www.equip.org/perspectives/are-there-apostles-and-prophets-today.
[161] Ephesians 4:11.

cannot be selected à la carte.[162] And if Jesus warned his apostles that they would need supernatural power in order to fulfill his commission,[163] either we are greater than the apostles and our natural talents greater than the Spirit's gifts, or the Great Commission ended along with the five-fold ministry, which would mean centuries of missionary efforts have been and continue to be unbiblical. Those who reject the apostles and prophets cannot have it both ways. And the result of trying to do so has left the church blind and immature.

In the book of Acts, Luke provides us with a vivid image of a church that is dysfunctional due to the suppression of the prophetic.

Around 60 A.D., a grain ship sailed along the shore of Crete. A gentle south wind suddenly exploded into one of hurricane force that swept down from the island.

> As we passed to the lee of a small island called Cauda, we were hardly able to make the lifeboat secure, so the men hoisted it aboard. Then they passed ropes under the ship itself to hold it together. Because they were afraid they would run aground on the sandbars of Syrtis, they lowered the sea anchor and let the ship be driven along.
>
> We took such a violent battering from the storm that the next day they began to throw the cargo overboard. On the third day, they threw the ship's tackle overboard with their own hands. When neither sun nor stars appeared for many days and the storm continued raging, we finally gave up all hope of being saved.[164]

Paul had warned them when they reached Fair Havens against continuing their journey to Rome.

> "Men, I can see that our voyage is going to be

---

[162] Matthew 5:18; 2 Timothy 3:16; Revelation 22:18-19.
[163] Acts 1:4-5.
[164] Acts 27:16-20.

disastrous and bring great loss to ship and cargo, and to our own lives also."

But the centurion, instead of listening to what Paul said, followed the advice of the pilot and of the owner of the ship.[165]

Paul was locked away below deck, blocked from sight, ignored by the captain and officers like New Testament apostles and prophets, locked away out of sight, ignored by church leaders. And like the ship that was taking Paul to Rome, the church has been blown into shallow waters and is in danger of running aground.

I was invited to a church once, along with a team of marketing experts, to evaluate its congregation and determine its level of maturity and cohesion and the effectiveness of its leadership. At the start, the Holy Spirit gave me a word of knowledge regarding the outcome. I wrote it down, sealed in an envelope, gave to the facilitator, and asked him not to open it until we were finished.

After several days of meetings and evaluating questionnaires, the marketing team met to discuss the results before presenting it to the church board. When they had finished presenting their recommendations for making the congregation more functional and effective, I leaned over and asked the facilitator if he still had the envelope. He did. I told him to open it, and he was visibly shocked at what he read. I asked him to read it aloud.

The conclusions of the marketers were similar to what I had written, and the facilitator was very happy that his experts had been able to discern the issues. But they could not see past the superficial issues and had no concept of what was happening in the spiritual realm.

When the facilitator asked me for my thoughts, I explained that Jesus had designed his church to be built on the foundation of the apostles and prophets and, even if the team's results were similar, they were reached by methods apart from God's pattern and intent. I warned that their solutions would fail.

---

[165] Ibid., v. 10-11.

He laughed at me and said his organization had performed this evaluation service for many churches and knew what it was doing.

> But the natural [unbelieving] man does not accept the things [the teachings and revelations] of the Spirit of God, for they are foolishness [absurd and illogical] to him; and he is incapable of understanding them, because they are spiritually discerned *and* appreciated, [and he is unqualified to judge spiritual matters].[166]

A year later, that church was gone, destroyed by the replacements and changes recommended by the high-priced professionals. Their solution had made a bad situation impossible and wounded many more people in the process.

But the church today is out of order, not only because it rejects its apostles and prophets, but also because other gift ministries are often misplaced or misused. For example, not every person in the pulpit necessarily has a pastoral gift. Some are actually teachers. Their congregations receive sound theology, but individual lives and relationships want for pastoral care. Other congregational leaders may actually be evangelists, who lead people to Christ and bring them into the church but whose flocks are unable to mature beyond salvation.

New Testament apostles

That the church refuses to recognize New Testament apostles and prophets does not mean, however, that the Holy Spirit is not still calling, anointing, and equipping them. So how do we recognize them? The way we recognize everyone in the kingdom of God—by their fruit.

I'll never forget the night that an African man knocked on my door in Durban. He told me the Holy Spirit directed him to me after his house had been burned down during recent riots. He said his name was Moses. I settled him in a room and went about my business.

---

[166] 1 Corinthians 2:14 AMP.

About four days later, the lady who attended our home came to me and said the man had not eaten for four days. I went to his room and found him prostate on the floor. I was afraid he had died.

He arose and said he had been lying before the Lord, waiting for instructions. He said the Holy Spirit told him to go to the Ladysmith area, around the Drakensburg Mountain range, to minister in one of the villages.

I asked how long it would take to get there by bicycle, and he said about a week. But it was only a few hours by truck, so I decided to drive him. At one point, we turned onto a goat trail that wound up the edge of the mountain and led to a river and what looked like a natural dam in the rocks where women were washing clothes.

Moses went over and spoke to them. When he finished, they balanced their washing bowls on their heads and went up the mountain path, beyond the reach of the truck.

I thought we were done and was ready to leave. But he said no, we were to wait there until they brought the men down from the village.

A few hours later, men began to trickle down from the mountain. When more than a hundred had gathered, Moses began to preach to them in Zulu, then lead them in a prayer of salvation.

By dusk, I was hungry. Surely we were done. But I was wrong again.

For two days, I watched as he ministered to the villagers, baptizing new Christians in the river and casting out demons by the authority of Jesus. It was amazing!

Okay, I thought, we're done now? But he said the Holy Spirit had told him the man chosen to lead the new flock had not appeared yet. So we waited.

Later that night, a little man came down and told Moses that the witchdoctor wanted him to leave because the spirits were upset. Surely, this was the time to leave. But Moses said the Holy Spirit told him to wait for the witchdoctor to come down.

Finally, while the new believers were dancing and singing, the witchdoctor arrived, spitting and making noises. The closer he got to Moses, the lower he got to the ground, until he was crawling on all fours, then on his belly, like a serpent. Moses bound the demons, preached to him about Jesus, and the witchdoctor was saved and immediately baptized in water. Moses spent the rest of the night with the former witchdoctor, praying with him and some of the other men and teaching them, while I, like the apostles at Gethsemane, fell asleep, exhausted.

Early the next morning, I awoke to find him still ministering and praying. The women had made fires in the night and were cooking *mieliepap* (maize grits) for all those who had stayed, which appeared to be everyone, because so many people were healed.

I asked Moses how he had come to know Jesus.

He told me that, as a young man around Ulundi, Kwa Zulu Natal, he was tending his father's cattle one day when two men came and stabbed him and took the cattle. He said he was put into a box for burial, and while the mourning procession walked to the burial site, a man came up to them and said he wanted to talk to the young boy in the box. Terrified, they put down the casket and ran away.

He said the man prayed and commanded him to live and to get up, so he did. The man spoke to him about Jesus, and after Moses had accepted Christ, the man took him down to the river and baptized him. He continued to minister the Word to him and left him a copy of the book of Luke, instructing him to read it and to pray and to do all that the Master did in that book. Then Moses lifted his shirt and showed me the scar over his heart from the fatal knife wound.

Before we left, Moses gave some final instructions to the leaders of the new church and promised to return soon.

After I came to America, I began looking for God's apostles, but I couldn't find any.

"When will I see the real apostles," I asked the Lord. But I had an unbiblical image in my mind of what an apostle should look like and how he should act.

The Holy Spirit reminded me of Moses, and I wept. I was very sad because I had failed to recognize the petite African man as an apostle. An evangelist? Sure. A healer? Absolutely. But I expected prophets to ride in fiery chariots, part seas, and stop planets in their course. I expected them to be famous, flamboyant, and philosophical. As I looked back, the Holy Spirit showed me that Moses was the real deal. Demons were subject to him,[167] people were healed,[168] and the authority he operated in was powerful.[169]

He wasn't educated,[170] and all he owned was a Bible and a bicycle. No home. No possessions.[171] *Just* his relationship with Jesus.[172]

New Testament prophets

And what of the New Testament prophets? They are here, too. But they look little like their Old Testament predecessors. For one thing, Old Testament prophets were often instructed to serve as a physical demonstration of God's *judgment*.

Isaiah had to walk around naked for three years.[173] Hosea was told to marry a prostitute.[174] And Ezekiel had to lie on his left side for more than a year and bake his bread using human excrement as fuel (until the Lord gave in and let him use cow dung instead).[175] New Testament prophets, on the other hand, declare God's *grace*. For the most part, Old Testament prophets were sent to the leaders of nations, while New Testament prophets are sent primarily to the church.

> These twelve Jesus sent out with the following instructions: "Do not go among the Gentiles or

---

[167] Luke 9:1; Matthew 10:1.
[168] Luke 9:1; 2 Corinthians 12:12.
[169] Luke 9:1; Matthew 10:1.
[170] Acts 4:13.
[171] Luke 9:3-4.
[172] Acts 4:13.
[173] Isaiah 20:3.
[174] Hosea 1:1-3.
[175] Ezekiel 4:1-15.

enter any town of the Samaritans. Go rather to the lost sheep of Israel.[176]

When a word was spoken over me that I would be a "prophet to the nations," it meant that I would serve in nations other than South Africa, not necessarily that I would be sent to presidents and prime ministers. The word *nations* also indicates ethnic groups.

Another difference is that Old Testament prophets were heroes.

There are two references in Scripture to The Book of Jashar,[177] which was "a collection of odes in praise of certain heroes of the theocracy, with historical notices of their achievements interwoven."[178] Such were the prophets of old.

Moses brought ten plagues upon Egypt, delivered Israel, parted the Red Sea, quenched the thirst of a nation with water that gushed out of rocks, and received the greatest body of law the world has ever known directly from the hand of God.

David killed a lion and a bear with his bare hands. Armed with nothing but a sling, he killed the giant Goliath and destroyed the Philistines, Ammonites, and Moabites, the Amalekites and Arameans, the army of Hadadezer and the Edomites. Isaiah destroyed the army of Sennacherib and turned back the sun. And Ezekiel proclaimed the destruction of Jerusalem and the temple, and they were destroyed. He proclaimed hope and restoration, and Israel became a nation again. Prophets in the Old Testament were bigger than life, "alpha" prophets, like Elijah, the "troubler of Israel."[179]

The prophetic mantle was passed from one to another, from Moses through Malachi. And as the prophetic office continued to progress, it grew and was transformed.

Elijah raised the dead, defeated the prophets of Baal, and consumed with fire the captains of King Ahaziah. Before Elijah was taken alive

---

[176] Matthew 10:5-6.
[177] Joshua 10:13 and 2 Samuel 1:17-18.
[178] Unger, p.555.
[179] 1 Kings 18:17.

into heaven, he asked Elisha, the man God had chosen as his successor, "Tell me, what can I do for you before I am taken from you?"

"Let me inherit a double portion of your spirit," Elisha replied, meaning the rightful inheritance of the firstborn.[180]

After his master left in a fiery chariot, Elisha picked up the mantel that had fallen from Elijah, struck the waters of the Jordan River, and they divided, just as the waters of the Red Sea had parted for Moses.

Elisha produced thirty-two miracles while he lived and one even after he had died.[181]

Malachi, the last of the alpha prophets, prophesied another transfer of prophetic power and authority, another passing of the baton.

> "See, I will send the prophet Elijah to you before
> that great and dreadful day of the LORD
> comes."[182]

When Jesus was baptized by his cousin, he revealed to his disciples that "all the Prophets and the Law prophesied until John. And if you are willing to accept it, he is the Elijah who was to come."[183]

The prophet appears once more, on the mount of transfiguration, where Jesus met with Elijah (representing the prophetic anointing) and Moses (representing the law).[184] I believe that, once again, the "Prophets and the Law" were passed on, this time to Jesus, who John was about to reveal to Israel as God's Chosen One,[185] in whom was the fulfillment of God's plan to redeem mankind.

> For God was pleased to have all his fullness dwell
> in him, and through him to reconcile to himself all

---

[180] Deuteronomy 21:17 KJV.
[181] 2 Kings 13:21.
[182] Malachi 4:5.
[183] Matthew 11:14.
[184] Matthew 17:1-3.
[185] John 1:34.

things, whether things on earth or things in heaven, by making peace through his blood, shed on the cross.[186]

Passing through the cross, the prophetic office experienced yet another metamorphosis. In contrast to the alpha prophets of the Old Testament, New Testament prophets are arguably even more powerful—baptized in the Holy Spirit, equipped with his incomparable gifts, and yielding his Christ-like fruit. But rather than being sent to kings, New Testament prophets are sent to the church to prepare the bride for her Groom.

God set the Old Testament prophets "over nations and kingdoms to uproot and tear down, to destroy and overthrow, to build and to plant."[187] This is still in the job description of the New Testament prophet. But instead of nations and kingdoms, he roots out sin, pulls down strongholds, demolishes "arguments and every pretension that sets itself up against the knowledge of God,"[188] and builds faith.

As the church suffers when it is not built upon the foundation of the apostles and prophets, it also suffers when the prophets do not work in unison with the apostles. Without this God-ordained synergy, the foundation is unstable and unable to bear its load.

The time has come for God's prophets to come forth and, with their co-laborers, the apostles, be restored to the church.

---

[186] Colossians 1:19-20.
[187] Jeremiah 1:10.
[188] 2 Corinthians 10:5.

CHAPTER FIVE
apostles and prophets

The function of the Prophet has almost invariably been that
of recovery. That implies that his business related to
something lost. That something, being absolutely essential
to God's full satisfaction, the dominant note of the Prophet
was one of dissatisfaction. And, there being the additional
factor that, for obvious reasons, the people were not
disposed to go the costly way of God's full purpose, the
Prophet was usually an unpopular person.[189]

~ T. Austin Sparks

God gave detailed and specific instructions for building the
Tabernacle.

For the entrance to the tent make a curtain of blue,
purple and scarlet yarn and finely twisted linen—
the work of an embroiderer. Make gold hooks for
this curtain and five posts of acacia wood overlaid
with gold. And cast five bronze bases for them.[190]

Or did he?

At first glance, it may appear that the Lord provided a clear blueprint
for the tent, furnishings, and utensils, but closer examination shows
it's really little more than a list of building materials and
measurements. We still have no idea what the finished product is
supposed to look like.

Give a dozen skilled embroiderers a quantity of "blue, purple, and

---

[189] Sparks, T. Austin (1888-1971), Prophetic Ministry: A Classic Study of the Nature of a
Prophet, 1954, p. xix.
[190] Exodus 26:36-37.

scarlet yarn and finely twisted linen," commission each to create a curtain, and you'll get a dozen different curtains. And what do acacia wood posts look like? Are they round, square, plain, carved? Is the gold overlay etched, flat, polished? And what exactly does a bronze base look like?

The Holy Spirit left all the details to the craftsmen.

God called out Bezalel and Oholiab—the Old Testament type and shadow of the New Testament apostle and prophet—to interpret and execute the pattern given to Moses for the Tabernacle. And the Holy Spirit filled them "with wisdom, with understanding, with knowledge and all kinds of skills—to make artistic designs..." Note that the Lord said *make* designs, not *copy* them.[191]

Imagine how the Tabernacle would have turned out without Bezalel and Oholiab—if Israel's carpenters, embroiderers, jewelers, and metalsmiths had only a parts list to guide them. The craftsmen needed architects, just as the church needs apostles and prophets.

> Surely the Sovereign LORD does nothing without revealing his plan to his servants the prophets.[192]

Interestingly, the pattern for the Tabernacle is the same as the pattern for the church.

> Son of man, tell the people of Israel all about the Temple so they'll be dismayed by their wayward lives. Get them to go over the layout. That will bring them up short. Show them the whole plan of the Temple, its ins and outs, the proportions, the regulations, and the laws. Draw a picture so they can see the design and meaning and live by its design and intent.[193]

Moses, Elijah, and others, while referred to as "prophets," were also types and shadows of New Testament apostles.

---

[191] Exodus 31:1-6.
[192] Amos 3:7.
[193] Ezekiel 43:10-11 MSG.

Then the angel who talked with me returned and woke me up, like someone awakened from sleep. He asked me, "What do you see?" I answered, "I see a solid gold lampstand with a bowl at the top and seven lamps on it, with seven channels to the lamps. *Also there are two olive trees by it, one on the right of the bowl and the other on its left....*" Then I asked the angel, "What are these two olive trees on the right and the left of the lampstand?" Again I asked him, "What are these two olive branches beside the two gold pipes that pour out golden oil?" He replied, "Do you not know what these are?" "No, my lord," I said. So he said,

"These are the two who are anointed to serve the Lord of all the earth."[194]

While theologians suggest several interpretations for the olive trees—Moses and Elijah, Israel and the church, or the archangels Michael and Gabriel—Dr. Bill Hamon sees yet another.

They could be a company of prophets and a company of apostles standing at Christ's right hand and left hand to co-labor with Him in bringing about the consummation of the Age of the Mortal Church of Jesus Christ and helping to establish God's kingdom on earth....

The apostle and prophet are the two that have the anointing to pour the oil of revelation into the bowl of the other fivefold ministers and leaders who are the pipes from which the golden oil of truth pours out to the whole church.[195]

I met a pastor once who was trying to understand the need for apostles and prophets in the development of the church. In seminary, he had been taught that the gifts and work of the Holy Spirit had ceased. I asked him if he had ever built a house, and he said yes.

---

[194] Zechariah 4:1-3;11-14, emphasis added.
[195] Hamon, 134-135.

"When did you hire the architect to draw up the plans?"

"Before I even had a concept of what we wanted to build."

I explained that, if he had built his house before he had the architect's plans and the required permits, he would have had to tear it down again because it would have been structurally unsound and in violation of a dozen building codes. It's the same thing with a church that has not been built upon the foundation of the apostles and prophets, according to the plan of the Chief Architect.

> "It is written," he said to them, "'My house will be called a house of prayer,' but you are making it 'a den of robbers.'"[196]

Jesus declared that the church he is building will be a house of prayer, a household of people in direct, ongoing communion with the Father. But God's people had commercialized it and turned it into a marketplace, not unlike the church today.

The first task of the prophet and apostle is to conform the church to God's original intent. That's why, if they are brought in *after* the church is already built, they are compelled by the Holy Spirit and by their anointing to dismantle the church, clear the debris, and rebuild it according to the pattern established by Christ.

> See, today I appoint you over nations and kingdoms to uproot and tear down, to destroy and overthrow, to build and to plant.[197]

graveyard prophet

While the functions of the apostle and prophet overlap at times, each is unique. Ezekiel's famous vision of the valley of dry bones provides an illustration of the apostolic function.

> The hand of the LORD was on me, and he brought me out by the Spirit of the LORD and set me in the

---

[196] Matthew 21:13.
[197] Jeremiah 1:10.

middle of a valley; it was full of bones. He led me back and forth among them, and I saw a great many bones on the floor of the valley, bones that were very dry. He asked me, "Son of man, can these bones live?"

I said, "Sovereign LORD, you alone know."

Then he said to me, "Prophesy to these bones and say to them, 'Dry bones, hear the word of the LORD! This is what the Sovereign LORD says to these bones: I will make breath enter you, and you will come to life. I will attach tendons to you and make flesh come upon you and cover you with skin; I will put breath in you, and you will come to life. Then you will know that I am the LORD.'"[198]

As Ezekiel prophesied over the dry bones, they began to rattle, shaking off dead flesh and debris. That's what the apostle does in a church that was not built according to God's pattern. He rattles things. He shakes off dead works, religion, and strongholds of lies, misinformation, and deceptions. He cleans out the goop and gunk, enabling the bones to fit together properly and in order.

Then, through the ministry of the apostle, the Holy Spirit breathes new life into the church, "until we all reach unity in the faith and in the knowledge of the Son of God and become mature, attaining to the whole measure of the fullness of Christ."[199]

Then he said to me, "Prophesy to the breath; prophesy, son of man, and say to it, 'This is what the Sovereign LORD says: Come, breath, from the four winds and breathe into these slain, that they may live.'" So I prophesied as he commanded me, and breath entered them; they came to life and stood up on their feet—a vast army.[200]

---

[198] Ezekiel 37:1-6.
[199] Ephesians 4:13.
[200] Ezekiel 37: 9-10.

An army, while appearing homogeneous, is efficiently diverse. It is a community of specialists with a wide range of skills and missions. So too, apostles understand that God's pattern looks different on each person and in each congregation, as well as within cultures and generations. Though God never changes,[201] he is wildly relational and interacts differently with me than he does with you, differently with a congregation in Cleveland and one in the Ozarks, differently with a woman and man, adult and child, Gen-Xer and Baby Boomer. His church and his kingdom are as varied as his creation.

Revealing the mysteries of God's kingdom is a key element of the apostolic ministry.

> Although I am less than the least of all the Lord's people, this grace was given me: to preach to the Gentiles the boundless riches of Christ, and *to make plain to everyone the administration of this mystery*, which for ages past was kept hidden in God, who created all things.[202]

God's kingdom is a mystery, often a paradox. It's Alice Through the Looking Glass, where the first are last, the persecuted pray for their persecutors, and the greatest are the servants of all.

God's kingdom is unnatural to the natural man. It's counterintuitive. And no wonder; it's ruled by a King whose thoughts and ways are higher than ours—higher, as in unfathomable and incomprehensible.

God has given his apostles authority to set things in order out of love for his people and a deep desire to see the body of Christ become the bride of Christ. The apostle aches for God's children. He longs for the light of revelation to click on in every believer because he shares God's heart.

> Jerusalem, Jerusalem, you who kill the prophets and stone those sent to you, how often I have longed to gather your children together, as a hen

---

[201] Malachi 3:6.
[202] Ephesians 3:8-9, emphasis added.

gathers her chicks under her wings, and you were not willing. Look, your house is left to you desolate. For I tell you, you will not see me again until you say, "Blessed is he who comes in the name of the Lord."[203]

If you can feel the hot tears searing Jesus' cheeks as he spoke these words, you have felt the heart of the apostle.

To the sinner, the apostle is a father, urging him to choose life,[204] assuring him that "the wrong desires that come into your life aren't anything new and different. Many others have faced exactly the same problems before you. And no temptation is irresistible. You can trust God to keep the temptation from becoming so strong that you can't stand up against it, for he has promised this and will do what he says. He will show you how to escape temptation's power so that you can bear up diligently against it."[205]

To the church, he is a servant.

> You know that the rulers of the Gentiles lord it over them, and their high officials exercise authority over them.
>
> Not so with you. Instead, whoever wants to become great among you must be your servant, and whoever wants to be first must be your slave—just as the Son of Man did not come to be served, but to serve, and to give his life as a ransom for many.[206]

While New Testament apostles no longer set and establish doctrine, which is permanently and immutably established in Scripture, they fiercely defend and protect it.

Apostles activate elders into their ministry.

---

[203] Matthew 23:37-39.
[204] Deuteronomy 30:19.
[205] 1 Corinthians 10:13 TLB.
[206] Matthew 20:25-28.

> The reason I left you in Crete was that you might put in order what was left unfinished and appoint elders in every town, as I directed you.[207]

And they impart gifts.

> God, whom I serve in my spirit in preaching the gospel of his Son, is my witness how constantly I remember you in my prayers at all times; and I pray that now at last by God's will the way may be opened for me to come to you. I long to see you so that I may impart to you some spiritual gift to make you strong—that is, that you and I may be mutually encouraged by each other's faith.[208]

After I visited a church in the south, the couple driving me to the airport explained to me why they didn't believe in the baptism of the Holy Spirit. As we pulled up to the curb at the airport, they asked if I would pray for their daughter. I said of course and asked if I could hold their hands and if they would stand in proxy for their daughter while I prayed. I asked the Holy Spirit to call her back into the kingdom of the Lord and empower and seal her with the baptism of the Holy Spirit. Then I left and got on the plane.

I arrived home to find a voicemail message from this couple. They were crying and talking at the same time—in tongues. When I returned their call, they were happy and laughing and told me that, driving home after they had dropped me at the airport, their front tire had blown, launching them across the median into oncoming traffic and over an embankment where the car rolled over twice. Still laughing, they said the funniest thing happened.

When they lost control of the car, they both had screamed, "Jesus help us!" and when they came to a stop, upside down in a ditch, they found themselves speaking in tongues.

While apostles share many functions, each has a unique, God-ordained sphere of influence and authority, a specific measure or

---

[207] Titus 1:5.
[208] Romans 1:9-12.

metron.[209] Authority and responsibility are inextricably linked. We are responsible for nothing beyond our authority, and we have no authority beyond our responsibility (this would be a good one to stick on your fridge, because it applies to a lot of other things in life, including parenting adult children).

> We do not dare to classify or compare ourselves with some who commend themselves. When they measure themselves by themselves and compare themselves with themselves, they are not wise. We, however, will not boast beyond proper limits, but will confine our boasting to the sphere of service God himself has assigned to us, a sphere that also includes you. We are not going too far in our boasting, as would be the case if we had not come to you, for we did get as far as you with the gospel of Christ. Neither do we go beyond our limits by boasting of work done by others. Our hope is that, as your faith continues to grow, our sphere of activity among you will greatly expand, so that we can preach the gospel in the regions beyond you.[210]

How then do we recognize true apostles? Surely not because someone puts "Apostle" in front of his name on a business card. One thing is to look for power.

> I persevered in demonstrating among you the marks of a true apostle, including signs, wonders and miracles.[211]

Keep in mind, however, that prophets and apostles grow into their call and anointing like anybody else and are given more power and authority only when they prove faithful with their current levels. Just as the church has yet to mature into the victorious bride of

---

[209] Strong, James, *The Exhaustive Concordance of The Bible*, 3358, An apparently primary word; a measure ("metre"), literally or figuratively; by implication, a limited portion (degree) – measure, 1980, Abingdon, Nashville. ISBN: 0-687-40030-9.
[210] 2 Corinthians 10:12-16.
[211] 2 Corinthians 12:12.

Revelation, we have yet to see the fullness and maturity of the fivefold ministry.

As important as power is evidence of love, humility, patience, and longsuffering.

> For it seems to me that God has put us apostles on display at the end of the procession, like those condemned to die in the arena. We have been made a spectacle to the whole universe, to angels as well as to human beings. We are fools for Christ, but you are so wise in Christ! We are weak, but you are strong! You are honored, we are dishonored!
>
> To this very hour we go hungry and thirsty, we are in rags, we are brutally treated, we are homeless. We work hard with our own hands. When we are cursed, we bless; when we are persecuted, we endure it; when we are slandered, we answer kindly. We have become the scum of the earth, the garbage of the world—right up to this moment. I am writing this not to shame you but to warn you as my dear children. Even if you had ten thousand guardians in Christ, you do not have many fathers, for in Christ Jesus I became your father through the gospel.
>
> Therefore I urge you to imitate me. For this reason I have sent to you Timothy, my son whom I love, who is faithful in the Lord. He will remind you of my way of life in Christ Jesus, which agrees with what I teach everywhere in every church.[212]

the prophetic side

T. Austin Sparks defined the essence of prophetic ministry as "going far beyond mere events, happenings, and dates."

---

[212] 1 Corinthians 4:9-17.

It is, he explained, "the ministry of spiritual interpretation…. It is the interpretation of everything from a spiritual standpoint; the bringing of the spiritual implications of things, past, present, and future before the people of God and giving them to understand the significance of things in their spiritual value and meaning."

The function of the prophetic ministry is "to hold things to the full thought of God, and therefore it is usually a reactionary thing. We usually find that the prophets arose as a reaction from God to the course and drift of things amongst His people; a call back, a re-declaration, a re-pronouncement of God's mind, a bringing into clear view again of the thoughts of God.[213]

The prophet knows the thoughts of God because he spends the lion's share of his ministry in the presence of the Lord. I don't mean he never leaves the house or that he lives in some kind of prophetic prayer closet with nothing but a lightbulb, a Bible, and a mini-fridge. I mean that, in addition to his private time with the Holy Spirit, the prophet develops a constant awareness of being in God's presence.

Wherever he goes, whatever he is doing, he is aware that God is walking with him and talking with him as he did with Adam in the cool of the day. Through this relationship and through many trials, he has earned the trust of the Lord. His ear is tuned to hear the voice of the Lord, his senses to recognize the face of the Lord.

And constant fellowship with the Holy Spirit deepens his profound affection for the Lord, which in turn saturates the prophet with the Father's profound affection for his children.

It is in God's presence that the prophet receives revelation, where God shares and crystalizes his thoughts through the Holy Spirit. Just as it is impossible to please God without faith, it is impossible to know and communicate his thoughts apart from revelation.

> I spoke to the prophets, gave them many visions
> and told parables through them.[214]

---

[213] Sparks, T. Austin (1888-1971), *Prophetic Ministry: A Classic Study of the Nature of a Prophet*, 1954, p. 2, 3.
[214] Hosea 12:10.

90

The expression of the prophetic ministry varies with the prophet, as he is enabled and led by the Spirit. One ministers mostly in words of wisdom and knowledge. Another in signs and wonders or dreams and visions. Like Ezra, a prophet may be a scribe and prophesy principally in writing. She may hear very specific words, images, or impressions from the Holy Spirit or see the kingdom in broader perspective, a bigger picture. Some prophets are very public, while the Lord keeps others hidden. One prophet's authority may be within a congregation, while the authority of others extends to churches, movements, or regions. And there are undoubtedly countless variations that we have yet to see until the prophetic is fully restored to the body of Christ.

In short, there is no formula for the office of a prophet. If there was a formula, who would need to seek God? Who would need the Holy Spirit, except to serve as a Holy Battery to provide the necessary power?

As with the apostolic and other five-fold offices, prophets are *called* to the office even before they are conceived.

> The word of the LORD came to me, saying, "Before I formed you in the womb I knew you, before you were born I set you apart; I appointed you as a prophet to the nations."[215]

We see a picture of the prophetic ministry in the interaction between Jesus and the Samaritan woman.

> So he came to a town in Samaria called Sychar, near the plot of ground Jacob had given to his son Joseph. Jacob's well was there, and Jesus, tired as he was from the journey, sat down by the well. It was about noon. When a Samaritan woman came to draw water, Jesus said to her, "Will you give me a drink?" (His disciples had gone into the town to buy food.) The Samaritan woman said to him, "You are a Jew and I am a Samaritan woman.

---

[215] Jeremiah 1:4-5.

How can you ask me for a drink?" (For Jews do not associate with Samaritans.)[216]

Like Jesus, the prophet breaks down racial, cultural, and religious barriers that have pulled apart the church for millennia. In the final agonizing hours before he went to the cross, Jesus prayed repeatedly that there would be no divisions among his Father's children.

> My prayer is not for them alone. I pray also for those who will believe in me through their message, that all of them may be one, Father, just as you are in me and I am in you. May they also be in us *so that the world may believe that you have sent me.*[217]

> I have given them the glory that you gave me, that they may be one as we are one—I in them and you in me—so that they may be brought to complete unity. *Then the world will know that you sent me and have loved them even as you have loved me.*[218]

If unity in the church assures the world that God sent his Son to redeem mankind and that he loves the world as he loves his Son, our *dis*unity testifies, even more loudly perhaps, that God did *not* send his Son to redeem mankind and that he does *not* love the world.

Fundamentally, the prophet's function is to reveal Christ and his kingdom.

Though Jesus was of them, among them, and the fulfillment of all their prophecies, Israel failed to recognize its Messiah. Ever since John the Baptist, prophets have labored to present Jesus to a world blinded by sin, just as he revealed himself to the Samaritan.

> Jesus answered her, "If you knew the gift of God and who it is that asks you for a drink, you would have

---

[216] John 4:5-9.
[217] John 17:20-21, emphasis added.
[218] Ibid., 22-23, emphasis added.

asked him and he would have given you living water."

"Sir," the woman said, "you have nothing to draw with and the well is deep. Where can you get this living water? Are you greater than our father Jacob, who gave us the well and drank from it himself, as did also his sons and his livestock?" Jesus answered, "Everyone who drinks this water will be thirsty again, but whoever drinks the water I give them will never thirst. Indeed, the water I give them will become in them a spring of water welling up to eternal life."[219]

The prophet foretells and forthtells[220] and speaks words of knowledge and wisdom to open the minds and hearts of recipients, enable them to see and receive truth, stir up the spiritual gifts inside them, and activate the ministry ordained for them by God.

The woman said to him, "Sir, give me this water so that I won't get thirsty and have to keep coming here to draw water." He told her, "Go, call your husband and come back."

"I have no husband," she replied.

Jesus said to her, "You are right when you say you have no husband. The fact is, you have had five husbands, and the man you now have is not your husband. What you have just said is quite true."[221]

Suddenly, the Samaritan woman received revelation concerning Jesus.

"Sir," the woman said, "I can see that you are a prophet."[222]

---

[219] John 4:10-14.
[220] *Foretell*: to reveal the future. *Forthtell*: to proclaim God's truth.
[221] John 4:15-18.
[222] Ibid., 19.

By the power of the Holy Spirit, the prophet also reveals the new order.

> Yet a time is coming and has now come when the true worshipers will worship the Father in the Spirit and in truth, for they are the kind of worshipers the Father seeks. God is spirit, and his worshipers must worship in the Spirit and in truth."
>
> The woman said, "I know that Messiah" (called Christ) "is coming. When he comes, he will explain everything to us."
>
> Then Jesus declared, "I, the one speaking to you—I am he."[223]

Once she had a revelation of her own condition and the identity of Jesus, the Samaritan woman turned her back on her old life and began another vocation. She went to tell those she knew and with whom she had influence what—and who—had happened to her and brought them before the Lord.

> Then, leaving her water jar, the woman went back to the town and said to the people, "Come, see a man who told me everything I ever did. Could this be the Messiah?" They came out of the town and made their way toward him.[224]

The Holy Spirit ministers through his prophets to bring about transformation, just as he did with King Saul.

> The Spirit of the LORD will come powerfully upon you, and you will prophesy with them; and you will be changed into a different person.[225]

Together, the apostles and prophets work to conform the saints into the likeness of Jesus Christ and expand God's kingdom on the earth.

---

[223] Ibid., 23-26.
[224] Ibid., 28-30.
[225] 1 Samuel 10:6.

CHAPTER SIX
the kingdom of God

The crucifixion was the shocking answer to the prayer that
God's kingdom would come on earth as in heaven.[226]

~ N.T. Wright

The function of the prophetic office is to advance the kingdom
of God—to preach the kingdom, reveal the kingdom to the
church, demonstrate the kingdom of God with power.

From his position inside the kingdom, the prophet draws the church.
From inside the church, he guides it deeper and deeper into God's
kingdom. But in order to function as God intends, the prophet must
first of all understand the kingdom of God.[227]

God's kingdom is all about the rule and reign of Jesus Christ. He is
the gate into the kingdom, by virtue of his suffering, death, burial,
and resurrection. When the Father calls us, we enter his kingdom by
repentance *through* Jesus *into* Jesus—into his suffering, death,
burial, and resurrection. Then, *with* Jesus, we rule and reign in this
life and throughout eternity as joint heirs of the kingdom of God.

And if [we are His] children, [then we are His]
heirs also: heirs of God and fellow heirs with
Christ [sharing His spiritual blessing and
inheritance], if indeed we share in His suffering
so that we may also share in His glory.[228]

---

[226] Wright, Nicholas Thomas, former Anglican Bishop of Durham, *Simply Jesus: A New Vision of Who He Was, What He Did, and Why He Matters*, HarperOne, 2011, p. 185, ISBN: 978-0-06-208439-2.
[227] Luke 8:10.
[228] Romans 8:17 AMP.

The kingdom of God is not synonymous with heaven. Heaven and earth will pass away,[229] but God's kingdom is forever, and forever increasing.

> ...the God of heaven will set up a kingdom that will never be destroyed, nor will it be left to another people. It will crush all those kingdoms and bring them to an end, but it will itself endure forever.[230]

> There will be no end to the increase of *His* government or of peace, on the throne of David and over his kingdom, to establish it and to uphold it with justice and righteousness from then on and forevermore. The zeal of the Lord of hosts will accomplish this.[231]

Nor is God's kingdom synonymous with any nation. Nationalism, at best, is patriotism. At its worst, it is idolatry.

In his internationally-acclaimed classic *The Screwtape Letters*, C.S. Lewis describes a correspondence from Hell between a retired old demon named Screwtape and his neophyte nephew Wormwood concerning the finer points of subtly diverting Christians from the faith via nationalism. Whether Wormwood's "patient" chooses pacifism or patriotism, he points out, is of little consequence.

> Whichever he adopts, your main task will be the same. Let him begin by treating the Patriotism or the Pacifism as a part of his religion. Then let him, under the influence of partisan spirit, come to regard it as the most important part.[232]

Screwtape goes on to describe the imperceptible transitions until the

---

[229] Matthew 24:35.
[230] Daniel 2:44
[231] Isaiah 9:7 NASB.
[232] Lewis, C.S., *The Screwtape Letters*, HarperCollins Publishers, 10 East 53rd Street, New York, NY 10022, 1942, p.42, ISBN: 978-0-06-170818-3.

world becomes "an end and faith a means," and "meetings, pamphlets, policies, movements, causes, and crusades matter more to him than prayers and sacraments and charity."

But, while nationalism should not be confused with the kingdom of God, the kingdom of God should—and inevitably does—impact nations.

After I was saved, I attended a very prophetic church, and a steady stream of prophetic speakers came from America and brought us the word of the Lord. It was a phenomenal time. We lived in the presence of the Lord. The gospel of the kingdom was being preached and our lives were being transformed, while our country seethed with bloody violence.[233] Thousands of people were killed in rioting. Property was destroyed. The media was shut down to keep the world from seeing what was happening.

Racial tension was at an all-time high. It was dangerous to go into the townships where all the killing was happening. But God's people were focused on Jesus and revealing him to a lost and dying world.

Empowered by his love and grace, men and women ventured into the most devastated areas to feed and minister to African families whose homes had been burned and who were prevented from getting on the trains to go to work.

We saw angels escort people through the barricades unnoticed. Many workers were protected and sustained by continual supernatural visitations. The message was clear: the kingdom of God had come, and it was time to reveal it to the lost.

In those days, a great revival broke out in the churches of South Africa. Rodney Howard-Browne[234] visited our church and the Holy

---

[233] *Apartheid* is an Afrikaans term, that literally means "aparthood." It was a brutal system of racial segregation that arguably began with the arrival of the Dutch East India Company in the seventeenth century, which established clear lines of separation between Europeans and Africans. The system was strictly codified after World War II when the National Party was elected to power. The last apartheid laws were abolished in 1991, but its final end is widely held to be the result of the 1994 general elections.

[234] Born in South Africa, evangelist Rodney Howard-Browne and his wife founded The River in Tampa Bay, Florida in 1996. He also heads Revival Ministries International.

Spirit wrecked our lives. The Holy Spirit moved so powerfully among children that schools had to close.

The Lord was reconciling his people to their destiny. National church leaders from many denominations met and prayed together. Led by the Spirit, they delivered the mandate of the Lord to the president and prime minister, warning of bloodshed in the streets if they did not release former president Nelson Mandela, declare that Africans were entitled to equal rights under the law, and strike down the segregation and curfew statutes.

The kingdom of God was revealed throughout the nation. It broke the power of racism and hatred. Nelson Mandela was released after twenty-seven years in prison, apartheid ended in South Africa, and Anglican Bishop Desmond Tutu headed the Truth and Reconciliation Commission which enabled victims of human rights violations to receive justice and the perpetrators to receive forgiveness.

Just as the kingdom of God is not synonymous with heaven, earth, or any nation, it also is not synonymous with the church.

The church is the body of Christ on earth, a living organism in which disciples of Jesus are joined together in accordance with the design created and executed by the Holy Spirit. The church inhabits and inherits God's kingdom.

Greater than both heaven and earth, the kingdom of God is so incomprehensible to mankind that even Jesus had to resort to simile to describe it, likening it to a treasure found in a field for which a man sold everything he owned in order to purchase the field and legally claim the treasure.[235]

In addition to being of incomparable value, God's kingdom is holy. No one unwholesome or dishonest—or religious—can enter.

> Not everyone who says to me, "Lord, Lord," will
> enter the kingdom of heaven, but only the one

---

[235] Matthew 13:44.

who does the will of my Father who is in heaven. Many will say to me on that day, "Lord, Lord, did we not prophesy in your name, and in your name drive out demons and in your name perform many miracles?" Then I will tell them plainly, "I never knew you. Away from me, you evildoers!"[236]

Instead, the kingdom of God will be populated by those who are poor in spirit[237] and persecuted because of righteousness.[238]

Kingdom citizens will be just and merciful, as illustrated by the parable of the king who forgave his servant's ponderous debt only to learn that the man had refused to forgive a petty debt owed by a fellow servant. Angry, the king reinstated the debt of the merciless servant and turned him over to the jailers.[239]

While the kingdom of God is all around us, it is also inside us, acting like yeast that works its way through the dough to make it rise and become a loaf of bread that fills and nourishes.[240] Understanding the nature and limitless scope of God's kingdom, however, only enables the prophet to preach it. To demonstrate it, the prophet relies upon the same supernatural power that raised Christ from the dead.

> For the kingdom of God is not a matter of talk but of power.[241]

But the power of the Holy Spirit is far more than his gifts. He also empowers us to love and forgive our enemies, as well as those close to us, and to control our appetites and passions.

> ...the kingdom of God is not eating and drinking, but righteousness and peace and joy in the Holy Spirit. For he who serves Christ in these things is acceptable to God and approved by men.[242]

---

[236] Matthew 7:21-23.
[237] Matthew 5:3.
[238] Matthew 5:10.
[239] Matthew 18:23.
[240] Luke 13:20-21.
[241] 1 Corinthians 4:20.
[242] Romans 14:17-18 NKJV.

Righteousness speaks of our restored relationship with our Father through Christ's atonement. Peace speaks of our position, seated with Christ in heavenly places.[243] Joy celebrates the fullness of our salvation—the assurance of our redemption, the comfort of our position in Christ, and the power to overcome our enemies—which expresses itself in praise and worship. The joy of the Lord is our strength.[244]

The kingdom of God is like a military objective, requiring us to overcome seemingly insurmountable obstacles and fierce opposition in order to obtain it.

> And from the days of John the Baptist until now the kingdom of heaven suffers violence, and the violent take it by force.[245]

Jesus speaks here of two kinds of violence. One is aimed at destroying the kingdom of God. The other is the force often required to acquire and abide in the kingdom.

On the one hand, the world and the kingdom of darkness fight to violently overthrow God's kingdom, targeting our relationship with him, our position in Christ, and the joy of our salvation.

On the other hand, the violent take it by force. In other words, Christians who are smitten with and wholly committed to Jesus Christ, are eager to sacrifice anything to advance the kingdom of God throughout the world, in the hearts of mankind, and in their own hearts.

They are like a mother trying to rescue her baby from a burning house. She is desperate, caring nothing for her own safety or the challenges and dangers that surround her. Her glands release adrenaline and noradrenaline. Her heart races. Respiration increases. Pupils dilate. Muscles contract. She throws aside every obstacle, even heavy furniture and flaming debris, doing whatever it takes to get her child to safety.

---

[243] Ephesians 2:6.
[244] Nehemiah 8:10.
[245] Matthew 11:12 NKJV.

Like any other kingdom, the kingdom of God has gates and doors. And we have been given the keys.

> I will give you the keys of the kingdom of heaven; whatever you bind on earth will be bound in heaven, and whatever you loose on earth will be loosed in heaven."[246]

Keys are entrusted only to those who have been granted the authority to lock and unlock the doors they fit.

If you visit the Tower of London just before ten any given evening, you can witness the historical gate-closing ritual known as the Ceremony of the Keys, a rite that has continued for about seven hundred years and which serves as a colorful metaphor for the keys to the kingdom of God.

> At exactly 21.52[247] the Chief Yeoman Warder (*Beefeater*[248]) of the Tower comes out of the Byward Tower,[249] dressed in red, carrying a candle lantern in one hand and the Queen's Keys in the other hand.

> He walks to Traitor's Gate[250] to meet members of the duty regiment Foot Guards who escort him throughout the ceremony. One soldier takes the lantern, and they walk in step to the outer gate. All guards and sentries on duty salute the Queen's Keys as they pass. The Warder locks the outer gate and they walk back to lock the oak gates of the Middle and Byward Towers.

---

[246] Matthew 16:19.

[247] 9:52 p.m.

[248] "The nickname 'Beef-eaters,' which is sometimes associated with the Yeomen of the Guard, had its origin in 1669, when Count Cosimo, grand duke of Tuscany, was in England, and, writing of the size and stature of this magnificent Guard, said, 'They are great eaters of beef, of which a very large ration is given them daily at the court, and they might be called Beef-eaters;'" Chisholm, Hugh, ed. (1911). "Yeomen of the Guard". Encyclopædia Britannica 28 (11th ed.). Cambridge University Press. pp. 916–918.

[249] Gatehouse of the Outer Ward of the Tower of London, next to the moat.

[250] The Traitors Gate is the water-gate entrance to the Tower of London, so named because of the number of prisoners accused of treason to pass through.

They then return along Water Lane towards the Wakefield Tower,[251] where in the deep shadows of the Bloody Tower[252] archway a sentry waits and watches.

As the Chief Warder and escort approach, the sentry's challenge rings out.

"Halt! Who comes there?"

"The Keys," replies the Chief Warder.

"Whose Keys?"

"Queen Elizabeth's Keys."

"Pass Queen Elizabeth's Keys. All's well."

All four men walk to the Bloody Tower archway and up towards the broadwalk steps where the main Guard is drawn up.

The Chief Yeoman Warder and escort halt at the foot of the steps and the officer in charge gives the command to the Guard and escort to present arms.

The Chief Yeoman Warder moves two paces forward, raises his Tudor bonnet high in the air and calls, "God preserve Queen Elizabeth."

The guard answers "Amen" exactly as the clock chimes 10 pm, and 'The Duty Drummer' sounds The Last Post on his bugle.

---

[251] Wakefield Tower once served as a private royal residence.

[252] "The Bloody Tower's gruesome name dates from the 1560s as it was associated with the mysterious disappearance of the Little Princes [Edward V of England (12) and Richard of Shrewsbury, Duke of York (9), the only sons of Edward IV and Elizabeth Woodville surviving at the time of their father's death in 1483] who were said to have been murdered by their uncle, Richard III." Historic Royal Palaces, The Tower of London, retrieved May 26, 2016 from http://www.hrp.org.uk/tower-of-london/history-and-stories/discover-the-towers/the-bloody-tower.

The Chief Yeoman Warder takes the keys back to the Queen's House, and the Guard is dismissed.[253]

In addition to binding the plans and activities of our enemy and releasing the grace and power of Christ, the keys to the kingdom of God unlock kingdom secrets.

> I will give you hidden treasures, riches stored in secret places, so that you may know that I am the LORD, the God of Israel, who summons you by name.[254]

The kingdom of God is greater than all the world's kingdoms combined, yet our Father gives it to us freely.

> Do not be afraid, little flock, for your Father has been pleased to give you the kingdom. Sell your possessions and give to the poor. Provide purses for yourselves that will not wear out, a treasure in heaven that will never fail, where no thief comes near and no moth destroys. For where your treasure is, there your heart will be also.[255]

The mission of the prophet, then, is to help the church see past the kingdoms of this world to the wonder and majesty of God's kingdom and God's King. As we do, "the things of earth will grow strangely dim in the light of his glory and grace."[256]

kingdoms of this world

As surely as there is a kingdom of God, there are kingdoms of this world. And the prophet must be able to clearly distinguish between the real and the counterfeit.

My daughter is very prophetic and at times finds herself at odds with

---

[253] The Tower of London, Ceremony of the Keys, http://changing-guard.com/ceremony-of-the-keys.html, Retrieved 05-20-16.

[254] Isaiah 45:3.

[255] Luke 12:32-34.

[256] Lemmel, Helen H., *Turn Your Eyes upon Jesus*, a hymn, 1922,

people who cannot believe that Jesus is the only way, truth, and life. They insist that it is enough to be good. And it is frustrating to her that they will not recognize the truth when she shows them.

Once, she was taken to task and hurt by a close friend who defended a political position that was antithetical to the kingdom of God.

Ministering to her, I explained that it's not that they will not see the truth but that they cannot. All the arguments and Internet postings, no matter how lengthy, well-reasoned, and true, cannot give sight to the blind.

> The person without the Spirit does not accept the things that come from the Spirit of God but considers them foolishness, and cannot understand them because they are discerned only through the Spirit.[257]

The kingdoms of this world are a stronghold of misinformation, and when we touch people with the truth, they protect their fortress, sometimes violently and hurtfully. They cannot love or accept those who disagree with them, because the love of God is not in them.[258]

"Your purpose and identity," I explained, "are not wrapped up in this world but in God's purpose in creating you. Instead of trying to defend yourself and win futile arguments, demonstrate God's love to those around you. Remember that you are royalty. View the kingdoms of the world from your vantage point seated beside the King of kings."

But what exactly are the kingdoms of this world?

> Again, the devil took him to a very high mountain and showed him all the kingdoms of the world and their splendor.[259]

They are alluring and capable of tempting even the Son of God. How

---

[257] 1 Corinthians 2:14.
[258] 1 John 2:15.
[259] Matthew 4:8.

much more so God's prophets!

> For we do not have a high priest who is unable to empathize with our weaknesses, but we have one who has been tempted in every way, just as we are—yet he did not sin.[260]

One worldly realm is the kingdom of influence.

> Now for some time a man named Simon had practiced sorcery in the city and amazed all the people of Samaria. He boasted that he was someone great, and all the people, both high and low, gave him their attention and exclaimed, "This man is rightly called the Great Power of God." They followed him because he had amazed them for a long time with his sorcery.[261]

It can be a heady experience to minister in gifts of healing and words of knowledge.

> A few days later, when Jesus again entered Capernaum, the people heard that he had come home. They gathered in such large numbers that there was no room left, not even outside the door, and he preached the word to them.[262]

When a prophet is besieged with pleas and lavished with expressions of gratitude and awe, he can be lured into believing that he had something to do with it or tempted to pocket some of the glory that belongs to the Holy Spirit.

There is also a kingdom of the air.

> As for you, you were dead in your transgressions and sins, in which you used to live when you followed the ways of this world and of the ruler of

---

[260] Hebrews 4:15.
[261] Acts 8:9-11.
[262] Mark 2:1-2.

the kingdom of the air, the spirit who is now at work in those who are disobedient.[263]

The "kingdom of the air" speaks of an invisible, supernatural kingdom of power and knowledge that is distinct from the supernatural kingdom of God.

Perhaps the greatest temptation for the prophet in this kingdom are the times when the Holy Spirit is silent or during seasons in which we are unable to sense his presence. Frustration, desperation, or the fear of man can tempt us to tap into other power sources.

> When Saul saw the Philistine army, he was afraid; terror filled his heart. He inquired of the LORD, but the LORD did not answer him by dreams or Urim or prophets.
>
> Saul then said to his attendants, "Find me a woman who is a medium, so I may go and inquire of her."[264]

Every kingdom has a king or ruler. The devil is the ruler of the kingdoms of this earth. Other demons rule as princes over regions, nations, and cities.

> "Relax, Daniel," he continued, "don't be afraid. From the moment you decided to humble yourself to receive understanding, your prayer was heard, and I set out to come to you. But I was waylaid by *the angel-prince of the kingdom of Persia* and was delayed for a good three weeks. But then Michael, one of the chief angel-princes, intervened to help me. I left him there with the prince of the kingdom of Persia."[265]

As the Old Testament offers types and shadows of New Testament realities, the cities judged by God offer a chilling picture of the fate

---

[263] Ephesians 2:1-2.
[264] 1 Samuel 28:5-7.
[265] Daniel 10:12-13 MSG, emphasis added.

of the kingdoms of this world.

> For thus says the Lord God of Israel to me: "Take this wine cup of fury from My hand, and cause all the nations, to whom I send you, to drink it. And they will drink and stagger and go mad because of the sword that I will send among them."
>
> Then I took the cup from the Lord's hand, and made all the nations drink, to whom the Lord had sent me: Jerusalem and the cities of Judah, its kings and its princes, to make them a desolation, an astonishment, a hissing, and a curse, as *it is* this day; Pharaoh king of Egypt, his servants, his princes, and all his people; all the mixed multitude, all the kings of the land of Uz, all the kings of the land of the Philistines (namely, Ashkelon, Gaza, Ekron, and the remnant of Ashdod); Edom, Moab, and the people of Ammon; all the kings of Tyre, all the kings of Sidon, and the kings of the coastlands which *are* across the sea; Dedan, Tema, Buz, and all *who are* in the farthest corners; all the kings of Arabia and all the kings of the mixed multitude who dwell in the desert; all the kings of Zimri, all the kings of Elam, and all the kings of the Medes; all the kings of the north, far and near, one with another; and *all the kingdoms of the world which are on the face of the earth.*[266]

Egypt was known in ancient times as *Kemet,* which means "the black land." Worldly kingdoms are kingdoms of darkness, no matter how much they sparkle and glitter. In Hebrew, Egypt is *Misrayim,* meaning "dual," probably referring to upper and lower Egypt, but it also speaks of double-mindedness. Citizens of the world lack faith, which James says makes them double-minded and unstable in all their ways.[267]

Uz is from a Hebrew word meaning *consultation* or *advice* and speaks of a realm where everyone does what is right in his own eyes.

---

[266] Jeremiah 25:15-26 NKJV, emphasis added.
[267] James 1:6-8 NKJV.

"Woe to the rebellious children," says the Lord, "Who take counsel, but not of Me, and who devise plans, but not of My Spirit, that they may add sin to sin; who walk to go down to Egypt, and have not asked My advice, to strengthen themselves in the strength of Pharaoh, and to trust in the shadow of Egypt!"[268]

Ashkelon means *weighing* and speaks of heaviness. Gaza means *stronghold* and speaks of a fortress built of ideas and beliefs that contradict God's word and wisdom and imprison instead of protect. Ekron means *extermination*. Ashdod means *ravager*. Notice a pattern here?

The kingdom of God versus the kingdoms of this world. Light versus darkness. Truth versus deception. Life versus death. Freedom versus bondage.

A prophet needs to relate to the kingdoms of the world from his position inside the kingdom of God. If he is positionally in the world, his perspective will be worldly, and he will rely on his own strengths and talents and lean on his own understanding, also known as sorcery.

So Saul died for his trespass which he committed against the LORD, because of the word of the LORD which he did not keep; and also because he asked counsel of a medium, making inquiry of it, and did not inquire of the LORD. Therefore He killed him and turned the kingdom to David the son of Jesse.[269]

The kingdom of God is experiential, not theoretical or theological. Inside is peace, whereas the world is in flux. Inside God's kingdom is assurance, whereas the world offers only confusion and doubt. The kingdom of the world is neither the flip side nor mirror image of God's kingdom, any more than the devil is the antithesis of God. The two are as incomparable as golf balls and galaxies.

---

[268] Isaiah 30:1-2 NKJV.
[269] 1 Chronicles 10:13-14 NASB.

So how could any man of God be lured to the Dark Side?

the spirits behind the scenes

In 1994, shortly after Melanie and I had moved to America from South Africa, I felt the presence of God drift away from me.

I fasted for a month, rested ten days and fasted for another month, rested ten days and fasted yet another month, all the time pleading with the Lord to show me what was resisting me.

"My son," he said, "the Prince of Liberty has declared war on you."

"God, you've got to give me wisdom," I said, "what or who is this Prince of Liberty?"

He told me it wasn't to be revealed to me at that time. So I wrote it down, put it away, and forgot about it.

Several years later, I visited the Nation's Capital. My spirit was so stirred! I came home that night, and the Spirit of the Lord took me up in a vision.

"Do you remember when I told you about the Prince of Liberty?"

"Yes, Lord."

"Now, I'm going to show you who this prince is."

The Lord showed me a majestic being who had been given authority for this age. He wore a bronze breastplate with the image of an ever-seeing eye. An inscription underneath said, "The Ancient Order." On his head was a bronze helmet with the image of the head of an eagle, and light came out of the side of the helmet. He wore white garments, had a white beard, and held a scroll with a seal upon it that was inscribed, "The Law of Sin and Death."

Then the Lord showed me a throne room filled with terror and deception, and I was aware of many schemes and plans and heard voices plotting against the kingdom of Christ. The Lord told me the room was named "Rulers in Wicked Places." And there were large marble pillars, many of which had fallen or been torn out by the foundations.

In the center of this darkness stood a great wooden throne with many others behind it. And above the thrones was written, "Fallen, Fallen Is Babylon."

I asked, "Lord, what does this mean?"

"This is the Prince of Light that has set himself against the kingdom of God in the Earth."

"Lord, what do you want me to do with this information?"

"I want you to write this down. I want you to make it known to my people what I'm about to reveal at this time."

Behind the throne of the Prince of Liberty were six other thrones, and six principalities sat on them. The Lord showed me that the principalities were joined together by a silver cord of covenant, of brotherhood against the kingdom of Christ. And from the Prince of Liberty were thirteen levels among the six principalities—demonic authorities that had been released against the body of Christ to bring confusion and war against the righteous of the Lord.

And the Lord said this prince and these principalities had been given authority for a season to cause the body of Christ to be tested and to bring tribulation.

The first principality held a gold chalice in one hand and a scale in the other, and the Lord said his name was Injustice. The Lord told me the chalice contained the blood of the saints and of unborn children that ratified the covenant the principality made with the prince. And the scales were weighted against the righteous. Together with the other powers, they used the law to bring men into bondage and to war against the grace of God that had been freely given. This principality, the Lord said, had committed many injustices against the saints and sent deceiving and lying spirits to steal and destroy our authority and power and to cripple our faith.

110

The principality had also conspired with the Spirit of Death to crush and kill the warriors of the Lord in order to leave this generation of saints without hope and direction by destroying the apostolic and prophetic movements through legalism and pride, so that men would reject the emerging apostles and prophets.

The second principality held a bag of money in one hand and in the other a sealed title, and his name was Mammon. The bag of money was the wealth of the world, and the Lord said the controlling spirits of Greed and Manipulation were contending against the body of Christ for our birthright. He said many Christian men had ignorantly joined themselves to this spirit and taken bribes and promises of success in place of their inheritance in Christ. In addition, lying spirits had established a deep, hidden strategy to lure men into a covenant with Mammon, who released principalities into the body of Christ to cause corruption and bring defilement through the powers of Greed, Debt, Murder, Jealousy, Strife, Suicide, Depression, and Idolatry. Many chosen of the Lord, driven by these powers, had lost their vision as their minds were flooded with worry, fear, and stress. I saw hopelessness displace praise for the Lord's provision. And the principality was laughing because he was choking the breath of God out of the saints.

The third principality was named Wickedness, and he had authority in high places and very high places. This wickedness had given over to intimidation, driven by pride and controlled by deception. Lying and deceitful spirits were released into the body of Christ, and I saw them perverting the mission and calling of God in men's lives.

The kingdom of the Prince of Liberty has been released and given authority and power at this time, which the Holy Spirit will use like a boot camp to train, strengthen, and mature the body of Christ. Nevertheless, many would fall.

The fourth principality was a big militant man in uniform. "This is the malicious Spirit of Religion that stands in the way of the body of Christ," the Lord explained. Religion held scrolls of the law in his hands, the power and authority of the law to destroy men's lives, binding them up in lies. Standing with this principality were others called the Doctrine of Demons and the Doctrine of Men, and behind them were cohorts of demons that were about to be released against the body of Christ. A Spirit of Deception would emerge from Religion that would deflect men from their walk with the Lord, some even at the cost of their lives.

The fifth principality was a good looking, highly esteemed gentleman. "This is the Prince of Intellectualism," said the Lord. "This principality is smart. He questions and checks everything to make sure it is all correct and balanced. He releases demons to twist and pervert the truth and to create confusion."

Then the Lord took me before the last principality seated on his throne and told me his name was Independence. Behind him was a large group of spirits, including Lust and Jezebel. Together, the principalities were mind-blocking demons tasked with blocking Truth. And without Truth, there is no freedom.

There is no authority except that which God has established. The authorities that exist have been established by God.[270] The Lord said he has given power and authority to the Prince of Liberty and the six principalities to sift the body of Christ, to separate the wheat from the chaff. This Prince will test the hearts of men, dividing the weak from the strong, the true from the false.

This is nothing to fear. God's people have power over the Prince of Liberty and all his principalities and demons. His name is the Prince of Peace. The Prince of Liberty has only six principalities; the Prince of Peace has twenty-four elders, [271] representing the full counsel of God.

> Then the seventh angel sounded: And there were loud voices in heaven, saying, "The kingdoms of this world have become *the kingdoms* of our Lord and of His Christ, and He shall reign forever and ever!"[272]

Thy kingdom come, thy will be done on earth as it is in heaven!

---

[270] Romans 13:1.
[271] Revelation 4:4.
[272] Revelation 11:15 NKJV.

CHAPTER SEVEN
prophetic anointing

God has anointed us, has sealed us, and has given us the
pledge, the foretaste, of the Spirit. If we are going to
minister something of Christ to others, we have to
experience Christ by the working of the cross, and the
working of the cross is for the anointing, the sealing, and the
pledge of the Spirit.[273]

~ Witness Lee

What exactly is an anointing? What's it for? What, if
anything, does it do? How do you get it? Can you lose it?
How do you know if you're anointed? How can you tell
if you're not?

The anointing is simply the impartation of the Anointed One. It
comes with salvation. You don't do anything to get it. It's not for
special people. It's part of the salvation package. While there is one
anointing, there are many expressions of the anointing. Sometimes
we sense it, sometimes we don't. But it's always there.

And surely I am with you always, to the very end
of the age."[274]

One time, at a conference, as I walked to the line of people who had
come forward for prayer, I felt virtue surge from deep inside and I
began speaking powerful words of knowledge and wisdom. It was
as though the Lord was there, expressing his profound love for my
brothers and sisters. I remember walking past people with nothing
to share with them, but the presence of the Lord brought them to
their knees, as though assuring them that they were his.

---

[273] Lee, Witness, *An Autobiography of a Person in Spirit*, Chapter One, Living Stream
Ministry, 1986, ISBN: 0-87083-261-1.
[274] Matthew 28:20.

113

Now it is God who makes both us and you stand firm in Christ. He anointed us, set his seal of ownership on us, and put his Spirit in our hearts as a deposit, guaranteeing what is to come.[275]

The anointing is virtue, the power to act.

And a woman having an issue of blood twelve years, which had spent all her living upon physicians, neither could be healed of any, came behind him, and touched the border of his garment: and immediately her issue of blood stanched.

And Jesus said, Who touched me?

When all denied, Peter and they that were with him said, Master, the multitude throng thee and press thee, and sayest thou, Who touched me?

And Jesus said, Somebody hath touched me: for *I perceive that virtue is gone out of me.*

And when the woman saw that she was not hid, she came trembling, and falling down before him, she declared unto him before all the people for what cause she had touched him, and how she was healed immediately.

And he said unto her, Daughter, be of good comfort: thy faith hath made thee whole; go in peace.[276]

The purpose of the anointing is to set us apart for service to God.

When you ordain Aaron and his sons as my priests, sprinkle them with some of this oil, and say to the people of Israel: *"This oil must always*

---

[275] 2 Corinthians 1:21-22.
[276] Luke 8:43-48 KJV, emphasis added.

be used in the ordination service of a priest. It is holy because it is dedicated to the Lord. So treat it as holy![277]

Prophets were anointed.

> Also, anoint Jehu son of Nimshi king over Israel, and anoint Elisha son of Shaphat from Abel Meholah to succeed you as prophet.[278]

So were kings.

> Then the men of Judah came to Hebron, and there they anointed David king over the tribe of Judah.[279]

Even Jesus, the King of all kings, was anointed.

> While he was in Bethany, reclining at the table in the home of Simon the Leper, a woman came with an alabaster jar of very expensive perfume, made of pure nard. She broke the jar and poured the perfume on his head. Some of those present were saying indignantly to one another, "Why this waste of perfume? It could have been sold for more than a year's wages and the money given to the poor." And they rebuked her harshly. "Leave her alone," said Jesus. "Why are you bothering her? She has done a beautiful thing to me. The poor you will always have with you, and you can help them any time you want.

> But you will not always have me. She did what she could. She poured perfume on my body beforehand to prepare for my burial. Truly I tell you, wherever the gospel is preached throughout the world, what she has done will also be told, in memory of her."[280]

---

[277] Exodus 30:30-32 CEV, emphasis added.
[278] 1 Kings 19:16-17.
[279] 2 Samuel 2:4.
[280] Mark 14:3-9.

The anointing is an indelible supernatural mark, manifest in a follower of Christ whenever the Holy Spirit illuminates his or her gift or office.

We have all observed the difference, for example, between someone who preaches head knowledge and one who imparts revelation. The latter is a manifestation of the anointing.

The proof of the pudding, as they say, is in the eating. Jesus put it another way:

> Watch out for false prophets. They come to you in sheep's clothing, but inwardly they are ferocious wolves. By their fruit you will recognize them. Do people pick grapes from thornbushes, or figs from thistles? Likewise, every good tree bears good fruit, but a bad tree bears bad fruit. A good tree cannot bear bad fruit, and a bad tree cannot bear good fruit. Every tree that does not bear good fruit is cut down and thrown into the fire. Thus, by their fruit you will recognize them.[281]

A person's anointing sometimes may be for multiple gifts or offices. In my life, for example, the apostolic anointing is stronger than the prophetic, as declared by many prophetic voices.

> Son, you have been seeing for some time now a grander call of God upon your life as not apostolic, but as an apostle. And you have attempted to step into that many times to serve my people. Some have received you; some have not. Let it not distract you from the call of God that is upon you. For your sphere is increasing…. Today, I brought you to Pittsburg, Pennsylvania to announce prophetically through my servant that you are seeing now a doubling of the measure…the sphere of influence. I no longer want you to say, "Well, I'm apostolic." I want you

---

[281] Matthew 7:15-20.

to see yourself as an apostle. It's time to name the baby!

At salvation, the anointing is a seed, a purpose. How much God is able to do with it, in and through our lives, depends on our relationship with him and our obedience and faithfulness to him.

CHAPTER EIGHT
hearing God's voice

I consider myself as the most wretched of men, full of sores and corruption, and who has committed all sorts of crimes against his King. Touched with a sensible regret, I confess to Him all my wickedness, I ask His forgiveness, I abandon myself in His hands that He may do what He pleases with me. The King, full of mercy and goodness, very far from chastising me, embraces me with love, makes me eat at His table, serves me with His own hands, gives me the key of His treasures; He converses and delights Himself with me incessantly, in a thousand and a thousand ways, and treats me in all respects as His favorite. It is thus I consider myself from time to time in His holy presence.... If sometimes my thoughts wander from it by necessity or infirmity, I am presently recalled by inward motions so charming and delicious that I am ashamed to mentioned them.[282]

~ Brother Lawrence

Someone once said, if you want to pack the pews, put "How to Hear God" on the marquee. Which would be okay, if it was intended to draw *unbelievers* into a church meeting. But it is troubling when it's addressed to followers of Jesus.

The works that I do in My Father's name, they bear witness of Me. But you do not believe, because you are not of My sheep, as I said to you. *My sheep hear My voice*, and I know them, and they follow Me.[283]

---

[282] Herman, Nicholas (Brother Lawrence), *The Practice of the Presence of God: Being Conversations and Letters of Nicholas Herman of Lorraine*, circa 1666, translated from the French, Fleming H. Revell Company, 1958, pp.36-37.
[283] John 10:25-27 NKJV, emphasis added.

Whoever belongs to God hears what God says. The reason you do not hear is that you do not belong to God.[284]

Sobering words.

the sound of his voice

God loves to speak to us. Among other things, he has wonderful secrets to share.

For whatever is hidden is meant to be disclosed, and whatever is concealed is meant to be brought out into the open. If anyone has ears to hear, let them hear.[285]

He also speaks to us to increase our faith.

So faith *comes* from hearing, and hearing by the word of Christ.[286]

God speaks to his children in many ways. To Moses, he spoke directly.

Now Moses used to take a tent and pitch it outside the camp some distance away, calling it the "tent of meeting." Anyone inquiring of the LORD would go to the tent of meeting outside the camp. And whenever Moses went out to the tent, all the people rose and stood at the entrances to their tents, watching Moses until he entered the tent.

As Moses went into the tent, the pillar of cloud would come down and stay at the entrance, while the LORD spoke with Moses. Whenever the people saw the pillar of cloud standing at the entrance to the tent, they all stood and worshiped, each at the

---

[284] John 8:47.
[285] Mark 4:22-23.
[286] Romans 10:17 NASB.

entrance to their tent. *The LORD would speak to Moses face to face, as one speaks to a friend.*[287]

Sometimes, God's voice sounds like thunder.

> "Now my soul is troubled, and what shall I say? 'Father, save me from this hour'? No, it was for this very reason I came to this hour. Father, glorify your name!" Then a voice came from heaven, "I have glorified it, and will glorify it again."
>
> The crowd that was there and heard it said it had thundered; others said an angel had spoken to him. [288]

It might be audible.

> The boy Samuel ministered before the LORD under Eli. In those days the word of the LORD was rare; there were not many visions. One night Eli, whose eyes were becoming so weak that he could barely see, was lying down in his usual place. The lamp of God had not yet gone out, and Samuel was lying down in the house of the LORD, where the ark of God was. Then the LORD called Samuel.
>
> Samuel answered, "Here I am." And he ran to Eli and said, "Here I am; you called me."
>
> But Eli said, "I did not call; go back and lie down." So he went and lay down.
>
> Again the LORD called, "Samuel!" And Samuel got up and went to Eli and said, "Here I am; you called me."
>
> "My son," Eli said, "I did not call; go back and lie down." Now Samuel did not yet know the LORD:

---

[287] Exodus 33:7-11, emphasis added.
[288] John 12:27-29.

The word of the LORD had not yet been revealed to him.

A third time the LORD called, "Samuel!" And Samuel got up and went to Eli and said, "Here I am; you called me." Then Eli realized that the LORD was calling the boy. So Eli told Samuel, "Go and lie down, and if he calls you, say, 'Speak, LORD, for your servant is listening.'" So Samuel went and lay down in his place.

The LORD came and stood there, calling as at the other times, "Samuel! Samuel!"

Then Samuel said, "Speak, for your servant is listening."[289]

Or his voice may be barely perceptible.

Then a great and powerful wind tore the mountains apart and shattered the rocks before the LORD, but the LORD was not in the wind. After the wind there was an earthquake, but the LORD was not in the earthquake. After the earthquake came a fire, but the LORD was not in the fire. And after the fire came a gentle whisper.[290]

He may communicate to us as a doorkeeper, opening doors he wants us to go through and locking doors he doesn't.

Paul and his companions traveled throughout the region of Phrygia and Galatia, having been kept by the Holy Spirit from preaching the word in the province of Asia. When they came to the border of Mysia, they tried to enter Bithynia, but the Spirit of Jesus would not allow them to. So they passed by Mysia and went down to Troas.[291]

---

[289] 1 Samuel 3:1-10.
[290] 1 Kings 19:11-12.
[291] Acts 16:6-8.

Sometimes, we can be reading his word and the Holy Spirit will give us fresh insight or understanding or make it "jump off the page" to get our attention and prompt us to spend some time thinking about it and asking him questions. Or as we're going about our business, a Scripture verse pops into our mind.

Shortly after surrendering my life to Christ, my wife Melanie and I suffered a bankruptcy and I desperately needed to hear the Lord. Unlike America, South Africa does not offer repayment and restructuring options. When you go bankrupt in South Africa, your creditors take everything. Every day, the Sheriff of the Courts came to confiscate more of our possessions.

Sick of being continually shamed, I prayed and asked the Lord to show me something in Scripture that would help us fight this constant intrusion. Exodus 14:13 came into my head. I had never even read it before.

> Moses answered the people, "Do not be afraid. Stand firm and you will see the deliverance the Lord will bring you today. The Egyptians you see today you will never see again."

I repeated that verse all day, began to praise the Lord for deliverance, and felt an unexplainable peace. The next day, the sheriff returned to take our car. I was angry and felt that God had broken his promise. Then the sheriff pulled me aside.

"I am a fellow Christian," he said. "I hate having to take your stuff, and I want to help you."

I asked him what he could do. He told me go to the Clerk of the Court and file a specific document that requested the judge to grant a stay against creditors repossessing our property. The next morning, I did exactly as the sheriff had said. I appeared before the judge, he granted the stay, the repossessions stopped, and the vessel God used was the very person who was taking our stuff!

But ours is a manifold God. The Scripture verse he gave me not only saved our remaining possessions but also increased our faith and encouraged us to go deeper into his Word and listen intentionally for his voice.

In addition to using Scripture, the Holy Spirit may speak to us in a vision.

> After this, the word of the LORD came to Abram in a vision: "Do not be afraid, Abram. I am your shield, your very great reward."
>
> But Abram said, "Sovereign LORD, what can you give me since I remain childless and the one who will inherit my estate is Eliezer of Damascus?" And Abram said, "You have given me no children; so a servant in my household will be my heir."
>
> Then the word of the LORD came to him: "This man will not be your heir, but a son who is your own flesh and blood will be your heir." He took him outside and said, "Look up at the sky and count the stars—if indeed you can count them." Then he said to him, "So shall your offspring be."
>
> Abram believed the LORD, and he credited it to him as righteousness.[292]

Sometimes, you just get a picture. It might look as real as if it was actually there in front of you, or it might be just an impression.

The first time the Holy Spirit spoke to me, I didn't really hear anything. I was praying for a man at church, and in my mind I saw a bottle. I didn't know what to make of it, so I just told him I saw a bottle over his life.

He started to cry and said he had battled for years with alcoholism, as had most of the members of his family. I prayed for him, and the Lord delivered him.

---

[292] Genesis 15:1-6.

I asked the Holy Spirit why he gave me nothing more substantive than a picture. He told me not to despise small beginnings,[293] and I understood that this was the first baby step in what was to be a lifelong learning experience.

The next time I spoke prophetically, I was standing in front of a young girl and heard the word "ballet." I repeated it to her, and she told me she was a prima ballerina with the Napac Dance Company of Durban.[294]

I was excited that I had heard so clearly a very simple word. Then the Lord said, "You saw the image and you heard the word. Now you are going to have to hear by faith and not by the outward appearance of those I send you to."

Sometimes, the Holy Spirit speaks to us in a dream.

> His mother Mary was pledged to be married to Joseph, but before they came together, she was found to be pregnant through the Holy Spirit. Because Joseph her husband was faithful to the law, and yet did not want to expose her to public disgrace, he had in mind to divorce her quietly.
>
> But after he had considered this, an angel of the Lord appeared to him in a dream and said, "Joseph son of David, do not be afraid to take Mary home as your wife, because what is conceived in her is from the Holy Spirit. She will give birth to a son, and you are to give him the name Jesus, because he will save his people from their sins."[295]

I dreamed once about overhearing a meeting between two men who were entering into a business agreement. In my spirit I knew this was not a good idea and would end in a legal battle. But I couldn't warn him because I'd never met him and had no idea who this new partner was. So I prayed against the assault on his business.

---

[293] Zechariah 4:10 New Living Translation.
[294] Now called The Playhouse Dance Company.
[295] Matthew 1:18-21.

About two weeks later I met a friend for lunch, and a man he brought with him was the man from my dream. Before we even ordered I said, "I had a dream about you, and you were in a business deal with a tall man with silver hair and blue eyes, and he walked with a limp. The Lord had me listen in on your negotiations and showed me he would be a bad business partner and would accuse you of fraud."

He looked stunned.

"That's exactly the case," he said. "I got myself into a business arrangement with a man who was robbing me. Then he sued me for fraud." He asked me what he should do.

I told him I had prayed against the assault on his business, and the Lord showed me that events would turn against his accuser, who would drop the case and walk away from the business.

"That would take a miracle," he said, laughing.

Three months later, he called and told me God had given him his miracle.

prophetic jargon

During World War II, Germany's virtually undecipherable Enigma encryption machines baffled the Allies and allowed Nazi U-boats to engage in a deadly shell game that was the scourge of the Atlantic.

The tide turned, however, when the mystery was solved by Polish code-breakers and a British team that included mathematician Alan Turing, who Captain Jerry Roberts credits with saving thousands of British lives.[296]

> In 1940/41 the German U-boats were sinking our food ships and our ships bringing in armaments left, right and centre, and there was nothing to stop this until Turing managed to break naval Enigma, as used by the U-boats. We then knew where the

---

[296] The incredible story has been immortalized in documentaries, motion pictures like *Enigma* and *The Imitation Game*, and the TV miniseries, *The Bletchley Circle*.

U-boats were positioned in the Atlantic and our convoys could avoid them. If that hadn't happened, it is entirely possible, even probable, that Britain would have been starved and would have lost the war.[297]

Encrypted files are the language, not only of espionage and modern electronic devices like laptops and cellphones, but also of the kingdom of God.

> The disciples came to him and asked, "Why do you speak to the people in parables?" He replied, "Because the knowledge of the secrets of the kingdom of heaven has been given to you, but not to them. Whoever has will be given more, and they will have an abundance. Whoever does not have, even what they have will be taken from them.
>
> This is why I speak to them in parables: 'Though seeing, they do not see; though hearing, they do not hear or understand.'"[298]

Sometimes the Holy Spirit gives us cyphers—objects, symbols, numbers, colors, etc.—to unlock and understand his hidden messages.

> To you it has been granted to know the mysteries of the kingdom of God...[299]

A few years ago, I told a man the Lord would bring him a buyer for his business by the New Year. Well, the year ended and another began with no buyer in sight. He called and asked what he should do, and I told him to pray and ask the Lord. Several weeks later, he called again and said the Holy Spirit told him the prospective buyer was using the Hebrew calendar instead of the Gregorian calendar.

---

[297] Roberts, Jerry, "People's War," BBC, 13 November 2014. German linguist Captain Jerry Roberts was a colleague of Turing at Bletchley Park.
[298] Matthew 13:10-13.
[299] Luke 8:10 NASB.

And before Rosh Hashanah,[300] the buyer came as promised.

God's cyphers are generally specific to the recipient. A dog might be one person's best friend, while at the same time ferocious and terrifying to another. Dates, too, can mean different things to different people. Red is calming to some, troubling to others.

Numbers can have biblical significance, literally or figuratively. The number "1" might direct you to the five books in Scripture that have only one chapter,[301] or it might refer to unity. Seven often represents completion (day of rest after creation, laps around Jericho, etc.). Twelve may imply divine arrangement (12 apostles, 12 tribes of Israel, the bride of Christ wears a crown with 12 stars, etc.).

Colors too may have significance: black for sin, white for purity, blue for the Holy Spirit. So might objects: fire for judgment or God's presence, water for the Holy Spirit, blood for life.

There are no rules. No absolutes. No codebook. We have to ask the Encoder and wait for his answer. Once again, the Holy Spirit is relational. He encrypts, not only to conceal his message but also to draw us to himself, because it pleases him to reveal his secrets to us. As prophets, we need to pay close attention to the way the Holy Spirit communicates with us, learn to recognize the terminology he uses, and enjoy the treasure hunt.

> It is the glory of God to conceal a matter; to search
> out a matter is the glory of kings.[302]

"Kings," by the way, include you.[303]

an audience of One

Knowing the many ways God speaks to us is not the same as hearing him. If we want to hear him, we need to listen for him.

---

[300] Jewish New Year, which begins on the first day of Tishrei, the first month of the Hebrew calendar, corresponding to September/October on the Gregorian calendar.
[301] Obadiah, Philemon, 2 John, 3 John, and Jude.
[302] Proverbs 25:2.
[303] Revelation 5:10.

Hearing God is intentional. We seek him out wherever he may be found—in Scripture, circumstances, creation, and in people. We pursue him and ambush him. And we respond when he invites us to his chamber, where our language is prayer and worship, the language of the beloved.

Moses worshiped the Lord in the Tabernacle. David spoke this love language as shepherd, prophet, warrior, and king. Today, we call it the Book of Psalms. Songs not authored by David were written by Asaph, whose sons prophesied not only with their voices but also through musical instruments.

> Moreover, David and the commanders of the army selected for the [temple] service some of the sons of Asaph, Heman, and Jeduthun, who were to prophesy with lyres, harps, and cymbals.[304]

Some imply from this verse that musical instruments can prophesy. We all can agree that trumpets have been used to communicate charges, retreats, taps, and reveille for millennia. But can the Holy Spirit actually prophesy through a keyboard, guitar, or drum kit? I believe the Holy Spirit can pretty much do whatever he wants. And if he enables people to interpret prophesies in tongues, why not triangles, tubas, and tom-toms? So, if you're a prophet and you play an instrument, play it to the Lord in his chamber. He will know what you're saying, and you might just hear him singing back to you in the harmonies of your strings or reeds.

Most of my life, I struggled with the idea of love, having experienced what I interpreted as love only when I did something good. It was a reward, it was conditional, and it quickly turned to something else when I did something bad. During one of my greatest battles, my mentor told me to go to the Lord for the answers I needed. But how could I get the Lord to love me like he loves everyone else? He was blessing them, but I never felt like I was blessed.

"Worship," Andrew said.[305]

---

[304] 1 Chronicles 25:1 AMP.
[305] I've changed his name to protect his privacy.

128

"How? I can't sing well, and I can't play an instrument, except the bagpipes, and I don't have a set anymore."

He laughed with me and said, "Just open your mouth and let the words come out." But I couldn't think of anything to say or sing that would help me worship the Lord. So Andrew told me to put on one of my favorite songs and sing it to the Lord.

I put on Simon and Garfunkel's *The Sound of Silence*. And by the time is was done, I was in tears. My heart was full, and my mind was racing, since the song was so appropriate and the lyrics spoke directly to my situation.

> And the people bowed and prayed
> To the neon God they made
> And the sign flashed out its warning
> And the words that it was forming
>
> And the sign said, "The words of the prophets
> Are written on the subway walls
> And tenement halls."
> And whispered in the sound of silence. [306]

Your song to the Lord doesn't have to be a "Christian" song. It just has to be a song that releases what is in your heart. My song of worship at that time was from a place of darkness and despair. But it carried me into the Lord's arms where I needed so desperately to be. It touched my deepest emotions, and I felt as though it touched the Lord's heart as well. And it is still a very special song to me. Today, I worship continually, singing whatever the Holy Spirit puts in my spirit to sing back to him. Day or night, I am always singing to him…my audience of One.

The Holy Spirit also speaks to us in dreams. And if we want to dream his dreams more often, we need to treat them as the word of the Lord.

Keep pencil and paper by your bed to copy his fleeting messages.

---

[306] Simon, Paul, *The Sound of Silence*, Columbia Records, New York City, 1964

Or dictate the dream into a voice recognition app on your smartphone or iPad, send it to yourself, and later cut and paste the dream into your prophetic journal (you keep a prophetic journal, right?)

If you don't hear anything immediately, it might be something you'll need in the future. So it's good to review the dreams and visions in your journal from time to time and ask the Holy Spirit what they mean and how you are to respond.

The bottom line is the more we hang out with the Holy Spirit, the more we will hear his voice and the better we'll be able to distinguish it from other voices.

When Melanie calls me, I don't have to ask who it is because we hang out together and I know her voice. And if somebody says something about her, I know immediately whether it's true because we live together. We've been through good and bad times together; faced overwhelming challenges together; loved, sacrificed, and forgiven our way through our marriage; and prayed and worshiped together.

Mostly, I know I'm hearing God's voice because I have an assurance in my spirit that trumps what I perceive with my senses or what I think in my mind. I know it's his voice when I have a witness in my spirit, as opposed to merely a thought in my head or a feeling. I know in my knower at the same time that my head may be full of doubt.

other voices

In the beginning, mankind heard only one Voice.

> The LORD God took the man and put him in the Garden of Eden to work it and take care of it. And the LORD God commanded the man, "You are free to eat from any tree in the garden; but you must not eat from the tree of the knowledge of good and evil, for when you eat from it you will certainly die."[307]

---

[307] Genesis 2:15-17.

Then, one day, we listened to another.

> Now the serpent was more crafty than any of the wild animals the LORD God had made. He said to the woman, "Did God really say, 'You must not eat from any tree in the garden'?"[308]

Since the Fall, mankind has had difficulty distinguishing God's voice from the cacophony of other voices. In the early 90s, after the fall of Romanian tyrant Nicolai Ceausescu, missionaries poured in from all over the world. Christian groups would enter a village, play their guitars, gather a crowd, and preach the gospel. Hundreds of people fell to their knees, wept, prayed to receive Jesus as their Savior, and gratefully accepted a Bible. A week or two later, Hare Krishnas, Mormons, or Jehovah's Witnesses would come through, and the villagers would do the same thing.

After half a century of atheistic communism, the people of Romania had a deep spiritual hunger but little or no spiritual discernment. They couldn't distinguish God's voice from any other.

syncretism

Syncretism is "the attempt or tendency to combine or reconcile differing beliefs, as in philosophy or religion,"[309] like the mixture of Christianity with animism in southern Sudan or the adoption of Shintō elements in Buddhism. *Chrislam* is another example—a jumble of Christianity and Islam that blurs the distinctions so much that some pastors today even provide their congregations with Qur'ans alongside the Bibles in the backs of their pews. Chrislam proponents maintain that the Isa of the Qur'an is the same as the biblical Jesus. One prominent religious leader goes so far as to insist that Islam, Christianity, and Judaism worship the same God and that the bloody conflicts between them are the result of "a deadly misunderstanding."[310]

---

[308] Genesis 3:1.

[309] *The American Heritage Dictionary of the English Language*, ed. William Morris, American Heritage Publishing Co., Inc., and Houghton Mifflin Company, 1969, p. 1304.

[310] Siljander, Mark D. *A Deadly Misunderstanding: A Congressman's Quest to Bridge the Muslim-Christian Divide*, HarperOne, 2008. Lending credibility to the congressman's theory, the foreword of the book is written by UN General Secretary Ban Ki-moon, and it

In the early days of my ministry, I attended every meeting that offered even a hint of the prophetic, so I could continually reassure myself that I was good with God. But like Eastern Europeans emerging from communism, I was unable to distinguish between the voice of the Lord and that of a familiar spirit.

Before we came to America, I had received many words assuring me of great success and promising that the Lord would use me in a profound way. I was excited and inspired and anxious to get on a plane as quickly as possible. When everything fell to pieces a few months after our arrival, I cried out to the Lord. The Lord said since I had listened to other voices, he had allowed them to influence me to make the transition without knowing his timing or exact destination. As he spoke, I realized that the voice I was hearing did not sound like the voices I had listened to at home.

Eventually, I was grateful that he had allowed me to be deceived in order to teach me a vital, though painful, lesson.[311]
Voices other than the Lord can come from anyone, even legitimate ministries.

1 Kings 13 offers a sobering warning to God's prophets.

A man of God was sent by the Lord to speak to King Jeroboam, who had sinned by erecting altars to false gods and establishing a priesthood for them. The Lord told him to deliver the message and return by a different route and warned him not to eat or drink there. But an old prophet, hearing all of this, set out to deceive his brother prophet. Why, the Bible doesn't say. That he was indeed a prophet is attested to by the fact that Scripture calls him a prophet and by later confirmation that everything the other prophet said to the king would come to pass.

Even a true prophet has the ability to prophesy falsely, because the spirit of the prophet is subject to the control of the prophet.[312] And

is endorsed by no lesser luminaries than former Secretary of State James A. Baker III and former US Attorney General Edwin Meese III.
[311] For another example of God sending deceiving spirits to correct or punish, see 1 Kings 22:19-22.
[312] 1 Corinthians 14:32.

even though the old man set out to deceive the messenger, the younger prophet had heard directly from the Lord, which always supersedes subsequent instructions or circumstances other than another word directly from the Lord.

Sometimes other voices are simply the result of insufficient knowledge of Scripture. Sadly, for example, many people today are unable to distinguish between God's Word and a sermon illustration or popular saying.

"Spare the rod and spoil the child," is not in the Bible. It was coined by British poet Samuel Butler.[313]

First Timothy 6:10 does not warn that "Money is the root of all evil;" it warns that "the *love* of money is a root of all *kinds* of evil." Huge difference! Cleanliness may indeed be next to godliness at Granny's house, but not at the Lord's.

And while the lion lying with the lamb is a charming metaphor, it's not scriptural. Isaiah's prophecy actually says that "the wolf will live with the lamb" and "the lion will eat straw like the ox."[314]

This may seem amusing in today's culture, but God takes a dimmer view.

> If anyone adds to these things, God will add to him the plagues that are written in this book; and if anyone takes away from the words of the book of this prophecy, God shall take away his part from the Book of Life, from the holy city, and from the things which are written in this book.[315]

standing stones

Everyone encounters seasons when he doesn't hear God. While it is often our own inability, sometimes he is simply silent, as during the four centuries between Malachi and the birth of Christ.

---

[313] Butler, Samuel, Hudibras. Part ii. Canto i. Line 843, 1664.
[314] Isaiah 11:6-7.
[315] Revelation 22:18-19 NKJV.

When you can't *hear* him, *remember* him.

> When the whole nation had finished crossing the Jordan, the LORD said to Joshua, "Choose twelve men from among the people, one from each tribe, and tell them to take up twelve stones from the middle of the Jordan, from right where the priests are standing, and carry them over with you and put them down at the place where you stay tonight."

> So Joshua called together the twelve men he had appointed from the Israelites, one from each tribe, and said to them, "Go over before the ark of the LORD your God into the middle of the Jordan. Each of you is to take up a stone on his shoulder, according to the number of the tribes of the Israelites, to serve as a sign among you. In the future, when your children ask you, 'What do these stones mean?' tell them that the flow of the Jordan was cut off before the ark of the covenant of the LORD. When it crossed the Jordan, the waters of the Jordan were cut off. These stones are to be a memorial to the people of Israel forever."[316]

"Standing stones" were frequently set up as memorials to the Lord, reminders of what he did in their lives, reminders of his love and mercy and power. What we call "the Lord's supper" is a type of standing stone.

> The Lord Jesus, on the night he was betrayed, took bread, and when he had given thanks, he broke it and said, "This is my body, which is for you; do this in remembrance of me." In the same way, after supper he took the cup, saying, "This cup is the new covenant in my blood; do this, whenever you drink it, in remembrance of me." For whenever you eat this bread and drink this cup, you proclaim the Lord's death until he comes.[317]

---

[316] Joshua 4:1-7.
[317] 1 Corinthians 11:23-26.

Likewise, Paul's instructions to Timothy were a type of standing stone.

> You then, my son, be strong in the grace that is in Christ Jesus. And the things you have heard me say in the presence of many witnesses entrust to reliable people who will also be qualified to teach others.... Remember Jesus Christ, raised from the dead, descended from David. This is my gospel...[318]

When you think you can go no further, crank up your memory.

> Remember those earlier days after you had received the light, when you endured in a great conflict full of suffering. Sometimes you were publicly exposed to insult and persecution; at other times you stood side by side with those who were so treated. You suffered along with those in prison and joyfully accepted the confiscation of your property, because you knew that you yourselves had better and lasting possessions. So do not throw away your confidence; it will be richly rewarded.[319]

Remember prophetic words you have received.

> But, dear friends, remember what the apostles of our Lord Jesus Christ foretold. They said to you, "In the last times there will be scoffers who will follow their own ungodly desires." These are the people who divide you, who follow mere natural instincts and do not have the Spirit.

> But you, dear friends, by building yourselves up in your most holy faith and praying in the Holy Spirit, keep yourselves in God's love as you wait for the mercy of our Lord Jesus Christ to bring you to eternal life. Be merciful to those who doubt; save others by snatching them from the fire; to others show mercy,

---

[318] 2 Timothy 2:1-2, 8.
[319] Hebrews 10:32-35.

135

mixed with fear—hating even the clothing stained by corrupted flesh.[320]

When you cannot hear, when you cannot see, when you cannot understand…remember.

Remember, therefore, what you have received and heard; hold it fast….[321]

---

[320] Jude 1:17-23.
[321] Revelation 3:3.

CHAPTER NINE
prophetic pitfalls

To seduce and thereby conquer a prophetic leader someone with a Jezebel spirit will seek to gain [his] favor. This individual will attempt to unite with a prophetic leader in the realm of the spirit, saying, "I'm just like you. I seem to know what you're thinking and feeling. We are kindred spirits." However, it will be a soulish tie that will attack the prophetic leader's mind, will, and emotions.... For men, this will often translate into sexual needs and desires.... Thus, their ability to keep a covenant is breached. Their influence and authority is forfeited; their ministry is destroyed, and God's Kingdom suffers a great loss.[322]

~ John Paul Jackson

I'm pretty sure there's a sign in heaven somewhere that reads:

Help Wanted

Apostles and Prophets. No experience necessary. Will train. Must be willing and able to endure stripes above measure, frequent imprisonment, stoning, perils of robbers, perils of countrymen, perils of unbelievers, perils in the city, perils in the wilderness, perils in the sea, perils among false brethren, weariness and toil, sleeplessness, hunger and thirst, cold and nakedness. Must exhibit a deep concern for all the churches. Equal Opportunity Employer.[323]

Call now, right?

---

[322] Jackson, John Paul, *The Veiled Ploy: Unmasking the Jezebel Spirit in the Church Today*, Streams Publications, 2001, p.37-38, ISBN: 1584830018. Used by Permission.
[323] 2 Corinthians 11:23-28 NKJV.

Prophets are perhaps the least favorite of the five-fold ministry.

Leaders throw them into prison or try to kill them. The people stone them. And pastors would rather eat broccoli than have a prophet in their congregation. In short, if God has called you to the prophetic, you're going to have problems. And though your attacker may have the face of a person, you'll find there's usually a demon in the background cheering him on.

I'm going to add a caution here about this chapter. While we need to recognize and understand our enemies, we do not need to dwell on them. I mention some of them only to give you a heads-up, not to immobilize you with fear. Think of it as commonsense advice, like locking your car when you park in a rough neighborhood, as opposed to a warning to stay home.

pride

Pride is a killer. Pride destroyed Lucifer and one third of the angels in heaven.[324] It destroyed Uzziah, king of Judah[325] and put a noose around Haman's neck.[326]

> Everyone who is proud in heart is an abomination to the Lord; assuredly, he will not be unpunished.[327]

Why?

> **Pride**, *n.* Inordinate self-esteem springing from a consciousness of worth; an unreasonable conceit of one's own superiority in talents, beauty, wealth, accomplishments, rank, or elevation in office, which manifests itself in lofty airs, distance, reserve, and often in contempt of others.[328]

If you aspire to be prophetic, Pride is one of your greatest enemies.

---

[324] Isaiah 14:12-21; Ezekiel 28:12-19; Revelation 12:3-9.
[325] 2 Chronicles 26:16-21.
[326] Esther 5:8-14.
[327] Proverbs 16:5 NASB.
[328] Webster, Noah, Vol. II, p. 42.

In my earlier days, the Lord opened doors for me to work with state and federal elected officials. When you get involved with men who wield that kind of power and authority, you're going to encounter the Spirit of Pride.

> Do not be misled: "Bad company corrupts good character."[329]

I'm not saying all elected officials are bad, only that the Spirit of Pride wields a powerful influence over governments.

The longer I worked with these officials, the more I began to sound like them. It was subtle at first, but it grew stronger and more entrenched, until I thought I was God's solution to the problems we were dealing with.

Little by little, I grew less and less interested in prayer and resolving things on my knees. I became compromised by Pride and Arrogance and lost the voice of the kingdom. I began to hate anyone who didn't believe as I did and slandered those with a different viewpoint.

After one trip to Washington, I was watching a political debate on TV. As the pundits argued, I found myself talking over them and becoming increasingly aggressive about why I was right.

That night when we went to bed, Melanie looked disturbed. When I asked what was the matter, she said, "I can't talk to you right now. We'll talk in the morning."

I felt as though I had just been sent to the principal's office. I lay awake trying to figure out why she seemed so upset with me and going over my argument to see if there might have been a flaw. Finally, morning came, and we had a cup of tea.

"Have you prayed yet today," Melanie asked me.

"I don't need to pray about anything," I said defensively. "I have all I need right here!"

---

[329] 1 Corinthians 15:33.

That's when she brought the hammer down. She got to her feet and pointed her finger at me.

"I don't know who you are anymore. You have become vile and arrogant, all that proceeds out of your mouth is rubbish. You have lost the prophetic voice. You have grieved me and our children, and I am sure that you have grieved the Holy Spirit with your venom and lack of honor and respect for those the Lord has placed in authority over the nation. As a prophet, you are supposed to cry out against injustice and mistreatment of the innocent, but you have agreed with the injustices by your associations. You don't know what spirit you are of! You are supposed to pray for these leaders, to be like Daniel to Nebuchadnezzar, and give them godly council, but you have sat at mixed tables,[330] and now you are powerless. I pray that the Lord will remove you from there and restore you to your original mandate by his grace!"

Well, where do you go from there? I was stunned, and hurt because everything Melanie said was true.

I had allowed myself to be seduced by Pride, and I felt ashamed.

Then the Lord reminded me that Vernon had spoken a word of caution to me about this very thing back in 1999. But the rarified air of power had made me forget. I pulled out the word and reread it.

> There are a lot of people being harassed and tormented because they've sat at a mixed table.
>
> They've sat at the table of the Lord and the table of demons. You're coming into a level of discernment that is going to scare people and draw people to you. There's going to be a snare set in you, if you're not careful, while you're flowing in the anointing, to do and to say things that will destroy people. You need to be careful because there literally is going to be life and death and you will see people fall dead.

---

[330] 1 Corinthians 10:21.

All I could do was weep. I could not contain the heaviness I felt. I repented to the Lord and to my wife and children and begged the Lord to remove me from this situation.

A few months later, the Holy Spirit released me from ministering in Washington. I let out a shout of relief as I began to see clearly again. The Lord spoke to me by that same prophet, saying, "I want you to be hidden." And today I am.

fear

Pride and fear go together like Leopold and Loeb.[331] I was afraid most of my life.

In the military, our slogan was, "Pain is the feeling you have when fear leaves your body." It was catchy, but it wasn't true.

When I began to grow in the Lord and the prophetic gift began to flow, I realized that fear had become my greatest enemy. It would hit me at the worst possible times, forcing me into fight-or-flight mode or completely paralyzing me.

Ironically, fear was alive and active in my life largely because of what I heard from others who were gifted in the prophetic. They warned me that the enemy would retaliate if I ministered in the Spirit. And whenever I was under attack, I told myself it was because the Lord was about to bless me and the enemy was trying to rob me of my blessing. The problem was that I never went to the Word to see what God had to say about it.

My fear became a superstition, until I was afraid of failure, afraid of man, afraid of rejection, afraid of loss, afraid of death. I hated the fear, yet I was enslaved to it, until I turned to my Bible.

> Have I not commanded you? Be strong and
> courageous. Do not be afraid; do not be

---

[331] In 1924, wealthy college students Nathan Leopold (19) and Richard Loeb (18) kidnapped and brutally murdered Bobby Franks (14). The pair admitted being driven by the thrill of the kill, their Übermensch delusions, and their aspiration to commit a "perfect crime" (Linder, Douglas O., *The Leopold and Loeb Trial: A Brief Account*, 1997).

discouraged, for the Lord your God will be with you wherever you go.[332]

Fear is simply the result of not believing the truth.

Jezebel

The spirit of Jezebel is another threat against the prophetic that is not to be taken lightly. The same spirit that murdered God's prophets thousands of years ago hates prophets today.

Jezebel was the wife of Ahab, king of Israel. She was the daughter of Ethbaal, king of the Sidonians, a people who worshiped Ashtoreth (the erotic deity of fertility) and Baal (the weather-god). Worship of these idols was perversely sexual and fatally seductive to Israel.

> [T]here was no one like Ahab who sold himself to do wickedness in the sight of the Lord, because Jezebel his wife stirred him up.[333]

Jezebel slaughtered every prophet of the Lord she could find and replaced them with nearly a thousand prophets of Baal and Ashtoreth.

Then the tide turned. God sent Elijah to challenge Baal's prophets to a supernatural duel. Both were to prepare a bull for sacrifice, and the deity that consumed the sacrifice would be acknowledged as the true God. Baal, however, seemed to be unavailable.

> At noon Elijah began to taunt them. "Shout louder!" he said. "Surely he is a god! Perhaps he is deep in thought, or busy, or traveling. Maybe he is sleeping and must be awakened."

> So they shouted louder and slashed themselves with swords and spears, as was their custom, until their blood flowed. Midday passed, and they continued their frantic prophesying until the time

---

[332] Joshua 1:9.
[333] 1 Kings 21:25 NKJV.

142

for the evening sacrifice. But there was no
response, no one answered, no one paid
attention.[334]

Showman that he was, when Elijah's turn came, he made what God
was about to do even more impressive by digging a trench around
the altar, filling it with water, and soaking both the bull and the
firewood.

Then the fire of the LORD fell and burned up the
sacrifice, the wood, the stones and the soil, and
also licked up the water in the trench. When all
the people saw this, they fell prostrate and cried,
"The LORD—he is God! The LORD—he is God!"

Then Elijah commanded them, "Seize the
prophets of Baal. Don't let anyone get away!"
They seized them, and Elijah had them brought
down to the Kishon Valley and slaughtered
there.[335]

After such a demonstration of God's power, Elijah must have been
elated. And we might be tempted to conclude that Jezebel wasn't so
much of a danger to prophets after all.

But then she threatened to kill him. Just a threat. And despite the
amazing, blood-pumping, God's-got-my-back victory he had just
experienced, Elijah took to his heels.

When he finally stopped running, he plopped down under a bush
and whined.

"I have had enough, LORD. Take my life; I am no
better than my ancestors."[336]

Little wonder that Jezebel believed herself to be omnipotent and
invincible.

---

[334] 1 Kings 18:27-29.
[335] Ibid., 38-40.
[336] Ibid., 19:4.

143

The good news for Elijah, as well as for New Testament prophets, is that she is not. God raised up Jehu, son of Jehoshaphat, anointed him king of Israel, and sent him to destroy the entire house of Ahab, beginning with Jezebel's royal son.

When Jehu arrived in Jezreel, the queen gussied herself up, posed erotically in the window of her palace, and tried to seduce him.

> Jehu looked up at the window and called, "Is there anybody up there on my side?" Two or three palace eunuchs looked out.
>
> He ordered, "Throw her down!" They threw her out the window. Her blood spattered the wall and the horses, and Jehu trampled her under his horse's hooves. Then Jehu went inside and ate his lunch. During lunch he gave orders, "Take care of that damned woman; give her a decent burial—she is, after all, a king's daughter."
>
> They went out to bury her, but there was nothing left of her but skull, feet, and hands. They came back and told Jehu. He said, "It's God's word, the word spoken by Elijah the Tishbite:
>
> In the field of Jezreel, dogs will eat Jezebel; the body of Jezebel will be like dog-droppings on the ground in Jezreel. Old friends and lovers will say, 'I wonder, is *this* Jezebel?'"[337]

Years ago, I was caught in the crossfire of a Naboth's vineyard-type of scenario. The name Naboth means *fruit*. Jezebel often attacks the fruit of a prophet's life. If she can cause bad fruit to grow—or make people believe the prophet's fruit is bad—she can persuade church leaders to cut down the tree and burn it.

> Watch out for false prophets. They come to you in sheep's clothing, but inwardly they are ferocious

---

[337] 2 Kings 9:32-36 MSG.

wolves. By their fruit you will recognize them. Do people pick grapes from thornbushes, or figs from thistles? Likewise, every good tree bears good fruit, but a bad tree bears bad fruit. A good tree cannot bear bad fruit, and a bad tree cannot bear good fruit. Every tree that does not bear good fruit is cut down and thrown into the fire.

Thus, by their fruit you will recognize them.[338]

Naboth had a beautiful vineyard close to the palace of Ahab, Jezebel's wimpy husband. Ahab wanted the vineyard, but Naboth refused.

"The Lord forbid," he told Ahab, "that I should give you the inheritance of my ancestors." Like a spoiled child, Ahab went to his room and threw a tantrum. When Jezebel found him and heard what had happened, she rounded up two false witnesses to testify against Naboth and had him stoned for blasphemy and treason.[339]

Several weeks after I had ministered at a particular church, I learned that a rumor about me was spreading through the region. I called the pastor to ask him about it, but the Jezebel spirit and the Accuser of the Brethren had been so crafty and the lie had been repeated so many times that everyone believed it to be true and no one would talk to me. No one even considered Matthew 18.

If your brother or sister sins, go and point out their fault, just between the two of you. If they listen to you, you have won them over.[340]

No one called or came to me. They just continued to spread the rumor. The more I tried to defend myself, the guiltier I appeared in their eyes.

Like Elijah, I went to ground. I cancelled ministry, prayed and fasted, and declared God's Word over myself and my reputation.

---

[338] Matthew 7:15-20.
[339] 1 Kings 21.
[340] Verse 15.

"[N]o weapon forged against you will prevail, and you will refute every tongue that accuses you. This is the heritage of the servants of the LORD, and this is their vindication from me," declares the LORD.[341]

I suffered from this Jezebel attack for four years. One day, I received a phone call from a friend who knew the situation. He said he and his wife had met the accusers at an art fair where they had an exhibit.In response to my friend's questions, they explained that they were satanists who were assigned to stir up demons in order to force the church where I had ministered to shut down. They explained that they wanted the building for their coven. They said they unleashed lying spirits against everyone who ministered at the church. They told them specifically about me, how they had told a lie about me, and they laughed at how gullible the church leaders had been—never investigating, believing the lie. No one had bothered to ask if the accusers were church members. No one thought it unusual that they had done the same thing to others who had come to minister there.

But where there is a Jezebel, God raises up a Jehu. That church no longer exists.

> Blessed are you when people insult you and persecute you, and falsely say all kinds of evil against you because of Me. Rejoice and be glad, for your reward in heaven is great; for in the same way they persecuted the prophets who were before you.[342]

deceptions

The Jezebel spirit, like her master Satan, excels in deception. Lies and half-truths are effective weapons in the devil's mission to steal, kill, and destroy.

When he lies, he speaks his native language, for

---

[341] Isaiah 54:17.
[342] Matthew 5:11-12.

he is a liar and the father of lies.[343]

If we don't want to be taken in by lies, we need to know the truth. And that is found only in Scripture. But knowing the word of God is not enough; we need to know the God of the word—Truth himself.[344] Scripture, like statistics, can easily be manipulated to support any conclusion. Pile up Bible verses that support the pre-tribulation rapture, and I'll build a pile that proves the rapture will come after the tribulation. Show that God is against capital punishment; I'll prove he's for it. As with the folks in Washington and on Wall Street and Madison Avenue, truth is how you spin it.

In the 90s, Christians were deceived by one of the biggest financial schemes in history. Greater Ministries International (GMI) scammed an estimated 18,000 individuals and ministries out of half a billion dollars with a con spun from the Bible itself. GMI founder Gerald Payne (sentenced to twenty-seven years for his conviction on nineteen counts of fraud, conspiracy, money-laundering, and related charges) said the idea for the scam—which promised to double your money in seventeen months or less—came to him when he read Luke 6:38.

> Give, and it will be given to you: good measure, pressed down, shaken together, and running over will be put into your bosom.
>
> For with the same measure that you use, it will be measured back to you.

He claimed it was a matching funds program. And it kinda looked that way, which is what kept federal authorities at bay for years.

"The feds say, 'We know you received over $200 million. Now, where did the rest come from?'" Payne boasted. "Isn't it beautiful how they do that?...I said, 'Haven't you heard about the loaves and the fishes?'"[345]

---

[343] John 8:44.
[344] John 14:6.
[345] Fechter, Michael, "Ministry sees profit in prophecy," *The Tampa Tribune*, August 16, 1999.

It doesn't take much torque to twist a parable. In the parable of the talents,[346] Jesus commended the servants who doubled their master's money. He even took the money from the third servant who buried it and gave it to the first servant. In this light, GMI's offer would appear to be good stewardship.

In the head, maybe, but not in the spirit. Is it likely that any of the duped ministry leaders inquired of the Holy Spirit and received a green light to gamble away the gifts sent to them by their donors? It was a get-rich-quick scheme, pure and simple, even if some might have had altruistic motives.

melee in the mind

The weakest point in each of us is behind our eyes. That's where the decisive battles take place between flesh and spirit.

> Those who live according to the flesh have their minds set on what the flesh desires; but those who live in accordance with the Spirit have their minds set on what the Spirit desires.
>
> The mind governed by the flesh is death, but the mind governed by the Spirit is life and peace.[347]

It's pretty straightforward. We're born with a mind governed by the flesh. The outcome is inevitable. As God's children, our task is to conform our mind to the mind of Christ, a mind led by the Spirit.

A mind conformed to the world, on the other hand, is filled with strongholds built out of misconceptions, disinformation, faulty logic, and unfulfilled expectations. The resulting worldview causes us to make bad choices.

For example, when their expectations were not met the way they expected, Abraham and Sarah drove Hagar and Ishmael into the desert. Bad choice. And to this day the descendants of Ishmael are a thorn in Israel's side.

---

[346] Matthew 25:14-30.
[347] Romans 8:5-6.

Robert E. Lee charged the Union stronghold at Gettysburg, based on a mindset that was influenced by a string of victories instead of on intelligence reports and the counsel of his officers. Bad choice.

Based on a mindset that Russians were an inferior race, Hitler sent more than three million troops plunging into Russia, expecting it to tumble like a dozen other countries.[348] Bad choice.

He grossly underestimated the Russians, and within six months "a quarter of all German troops in Russia, some 750,000 men, were either dead, wounded, missing, or ill."[349]

If we want to make sound choices, we need to tear down the strongholds in our mind by changing the way we think.

> You were taught, with regard to your former way of life, to put off your old self, which is being corrupted by its deceitful desires; *to be made new in the attitude of your minds*; and to put on the new self, created to be like God in true righteousness and holiness.[350]

Throughout my childhood and into adulthood, my thoughts burned with anger, violence, and rejection. After I gave my life to Jesus, I went through nearly two years of discipleship and deliverance and was doing wonderfully. The Lord was giving me words of wisdom and knowledge, and I was prophesying and truly enjoying hearing from the Lord.

One day, on the way to church, Melanie and I stopped at a grocery store to get juice for our daughter. When I came out, I saw about ten men attacking a lone police officer. I ran to my car and grabbed a hammer out of the trunk.

A soldier was standing by, just watching the attack. I called to him to help, but he said, "Not my problem," which made me furious.

---

[348] "Attack on Russia," The History Place™, retrieved 06-16-16 from http://www.history place.com/worldwar2/defeat/attack-russia.htm.
[349] Ibid.
[350] Ephesians 4:22-24, emphasis added.

Filled with rage and a burning desire to kill them, I ran across the road, hammer in hand, and laid into those guys.

After a few minutes, half a dozen police cars pulled up, jumped into the fray, and arrested the men. They thanked me for my service, and off I went to church.

During praise and worship, I began to feel remorse as I recognized that my mind was still far from renewed. To the police, I was a hero. Helping the officer was the right thing to do. I was also justified in being angry at the soldier who just stood there as the man was being beaten. But my attitude was wrong. I wasn't motivated by love for the officer; I was motivated by hatred and a desire to kill his assailants.

> In your anger, do not sin...[351]

At that time in my life, my mind was still carnal.

Carnal thinking in a prophet is like static on a radio. It interferes with the transmission of the Holy Spirit. Prophesying after the flesh perverts the word of the Lord and tries to make it conform to what we see, how a person is dressed or behaves, or what we know or think we know about a situation. It muddles our ministry.

Jesus was addressing Peter's carnal mind, not Peter himself, when the fisherman rebuked him for prophesying his death and resurrection.

> "Get behind me, Satan! You are a stumbling block
> to me; you do not have in mind the concerns of
> God, but merely human concerns."[352]

The natural mind is not only carnal, but also futile.

> So this I say, and affirm together with the Lord,
> that you walk no longer just as the Gentiles also
> walk, in the futility of their mind, being darkened

---

[351] Ibid., verse 26.
[352] Matthew 16:23.

in their understanding, excluded from the life of God because of the ignorance that is in them, because of the hardness of their heart; and they, having become callous, have given themselves over to sensuality for the practice of every kind of impurity with greediness.[353]

A futile mind should not expect to hear from God. Sexual impurity, greed, and covetousness are part of the package when we're born. But when we're born again, they need to go.

It breaks my heart to hear Christians boasting that God is dealing with them about such-and-such a sin month after month. And a year later, they're still saying that God is dealing with them about the same issue, as though it is evidence of intimacy with him.

It has been rightly said that we need to keep short accounts with God. We do well to follow David's example as he opened himself regularly to the Holy Spirit for inspection.

Search me, God, and know my heart; test me and know my anxious thoughts. See if there is any offensive way in me, and lead me in the way everlasting.[354]

As soon as the Spirit points out something that stands between us and him or that hinders us in doing his will, we need to crush it.

For godly sorrow produces repentance *leading* to salvation, not to be regretted; but the sorrow of the world produces death. For observe this very thing, that you sorrowed in a godly manner: What diligence it produced in you, *what clearing of yourselves, what* indignation, *what* fear, *what* vehement desire, *what* zeal, *what* vindication! In all *things* you proved yourselves to be clear in this matter.[355]

---

[353] Ephesians 4:17-19 NASB.
[354] Psalm 139:23-24.
[355] 2 Corinthians 7:10-11 NKJV.

Hear the passion, the intensity? Repentance is active, ruthless, not something we get around to by and by. God will pursue us only so long. If we insist on protecting our pet sins, he will leave us to it.

> Furthermore, just as they did not think it worthwhile to retain the knowledge of God, so God gave them over to a depraved mind, so that they do what ought not to be done.[356]

That ought to terrify us. Repentance needs to be urgent, frequent, and unqualified. But prevention is better than repentance. We need to intentionally and proactively filter our minds.

> To the pure, all things are pure, but to those who are corrupted and do not believe, nothing is pure. In fact, both their minds and consciences are corrupted.[357]

During the 50's, in the early days of computer science, GIGO was a common acronym. It meant "Garbage In, Garbage Out." Or in the words of 19th century French physician Anthelme Brillat-Savarin: *Dis-moi ce que tu manges, je te dirai ce que tu es*,[358] loosely translated, "you are what you eat." Our senses are assaulted every day by the world's ideas, beliefs, and behavior. In addition to the rest of the armor of God,[359] we desperately need the helmet of salvation to protect our thought life. As we regularly absorb Scripture, we fill our minds with God's words, ways, and thoughts, displacing the wisdom of the world, like a ship displaces water, leaving room for nothing but the ship.

nationalism

The Spirit of Nationalism can turn the hearts of Christians from God to country and cause us to seek political solutions to spiritual problems. The prophet is especially susceptible because he or she is

---

[356] Romans 1:28.
[357] Titus 1:15.
[358] Hamblin, James, "1922: Strength and Vigor Depend on What You Eat," *Atlantic Monthly*, April 1, 2014.
[359] Ephesians 6:10-18.

wired by God to be uniquely sensitive to and aggressive against injustice and unrighteousness.

Misdirected passion has been the downfall of many men and women of God. And, like the Spirit of Pride, the Spirit of Nationalism can sneak up on you.

The Light and the Glory is an historical account of the founding of America. It tells of the planting season of 1623 following a terrible famine the previous year. Prior to this, the Pilgrims had labored in a common field, shared in the harvest, and nearly starved to death. For the second planting, the Pilgrims were each allowed individual lots for their own use. But the dry spell between the first and second planting turned into a record-breaking drought.

The Pilgrims began to fast and pray and examine their hearts, and they soon realized that they had allowed their faith to shift subtly from God to their ability to provide for themselves. So God had drawn their attention to their misplaced trust which, if left unchecked, could have meant their ruin. And with their repentance came the rain.

> "...without either wind or thunder, or any violence, and by degrees in that abundance as that the earth was thoroughly wet and soaked therewith. Which did so apparently revive and quicken the decayed corn and other fruits, as was wonderful to see and made the Indians astonished to behold."[360]

Like the Pilgrims, we can subtly shift our trust from God to government. When problems get worse, we blame the politicians instead of inviting the Holy Spirit to inspect our own hearts.

disappointment

Someone who obviously had a history with the Lord once quipped, "God is not always on time, but he's never late." God lives outside

---

[360] Bradford, William, *Of Plimouth Plantation*, Wright and Potter edition, 1899, p.171.

of time, which gives him an annoying flexibility.

We all generate expectations, especially of God. That's good. We should expect him to fulfill his promises. We should expect him to always act towards us out of love. We should expect that he will never allow us to be tempted beyond what we can bear and that he will always give us a way out so that we can stand up under it.[361]

We should *expect* God but never *anticipate* him. The former means to wait for, to entertain at least a slight belief that an event will happen; the latter means to take before the proper time or to act before another so as to prevent him. In other words, we must believe and wait for God to act (intervene or keep his promise), but we must not get ahead of him and thereby prevent him from acting in his perfect timing.

We also get into trouble when our expectations are based on our opinion of how he will do it and when. Or we forget that God's thoughts and ways are exponentially higher than ours and think that if *we* can't see a way out of a difficulty, *he* can't either, which is silly, but we do it.

The Bible calls unmet expectations "hope deferred".

> Hope deferred makes the heart sick, but a longing fulfilled is a tree of life.[362]

There are times when the Lord hides things from his prophets, as he did about the Shunammite's son.

> But the woman became pregnant, and the next year about that same time she gave birth to a son, just as Elisha had told her.
>
> The child grew, and one day he went out to his father, who was with the reapers. He said to his father, "My head! My head!" His father told a servant, "Carry him to his mother."

---

[361] 1 Corinthians 10:13.
[362] Proverbs 13:12.

154

After the servant had lifted him up and carried him to his mother, the boy sat on her lap until noon, and then he died. She went up and laid him on the bed of the man of God, then shut the door and went out....

When he saw her in the distance, the man of God said to his servant Gehazi, "Look! There's the Shunammite! Run to meet her and ask her, 'Are you all right? Is your husband all right? Is your child all right?'"

"Everything is all right," she said.

When she reached the man of God at the mountain, she took hold of his feet. Gehazi came over to push her away, but the man of God said, "Leave her alone! She is in bitter distress, but the LORD has hidden it from me and has not told me why."

"Did I ask you for a son, my lord?" she said. "Didn't I tell you, 'Don't raise my hopes'?"[363]

There are times when the prophet obeys the Lord, yet does not get the expected result.

Elisha said to Gehazi, "Tuck your cloak into your belt, take my staff in your hand and run. Don't greet anyone you meet, and if anyone greets you, do not answer. Lay my staff on the boy's face."

But the child's mother said, "As surely as the LORD lives and as you live, I will not leave you." So he got up and followed her.

Gehazi went on ahead and laid the staff on the boy's face, but there was no sound or response. So

---

[363] 2 Kings 4:17-21; 25-28.

Gehazi went back to meet Elisha and told him, "The boy has not awakened."[364]

And there are times when the prophet obeys the Lord and has to press through as the Holy Spirit leads him, just as Jesus did with the blind man at Bethsaida, in order to see the desired result.

> They came to Bethsaida, and some people brought a blind man and begged Jesus to touch him. He took the blind man by the hand and led him outside the village. When he had spit on the man's eyes and put his hands on him, Jesus asked, "Do you see anything?" He looked up and said, "I see people; they look like trees walking around." Once more Jesus put his hands on the man's eyes. Then his eyes were opened, his sight was restored, and he saw everything clearly.[365]

Disappointment is not a sin. Moses was saved out of the crocodile-infested Nile, adopted by Pharaoh's daughter, and destined for greatness,[366] then suddenly found himself herding sheep in the desert.[367]

Disappointed? Possibly. But it wasn't sin.

The danger of disappointment is that it can lead to discouragement, pull you into disillusionment, and spiral down into depression and unbelief. Now, you've got sin.

One of my greatest disappointments came when I believed that the Lord was going to heal a close friend of ours who had a sudden onset of cancer. The Holy Spirit told me that the cancer was not unto death but unto the glory of the Lord.

I had total confidence in the word and prayed constantly to call it forth. Soon, her healing began to manifest and everyone rejoiced.

---

[364] Ibid., 29-31.
[365] Mark 8:22-25.
[366] Exodus 2:1-10.
[367] Ibid., 11-3:1.

After a while, though, she developed a cough, which turned into pneumonia and took her life while I sat there believing she would be healed again.

I was devastated and disappointed with the Lord for not doing what the prophetic word had said.

For weeks, I wrestled with the disappointment. Then I sat down and poured out my heart to a friend, who cried with me and said I shouldn't feel guilt or shame, since I don't hold the keys to death.

I repented and made my peace with God, but I still had a hole in my heart and had to fight hard to keep from cycling down into depression or despair.

One night, while I slept, the Lord took my pain, and I awoke feeling whole again.

Several days later, I had a dream and saw our friend healed and singing and walking through a field of green wheat under a bright sun. She was smiling and laughing, and I knew she was healed.

Divine protection is another promise that can create expectations.

When Jesus talked to his disciples about the end times, he promised what sounded like unqualified protection against harm.

> But before all this, they will seize you and persecute you. They will hand you over to synagogues and put you in prison, and you will be brought before kings and governors, and all on account of my name. And so you will bear testimony to me. But make up your mind not to worry beforehand how you will defend yourselves. For I will give you words and wisdom that none of your adversaries will be able to resist or contradict.
>
> You will be betrayed even by parents, brothers and sisters, relatives and friends, and they will put

some of you to death. Everyone will hate you because of me. *But not a hair of your head will perish.*[368]

Some of his disciples must have grabbed onto this and might have experienced disappointment when they were arrested, beaten, and imprisoned. And we do the same thing today, holding God's feet to the fire, and when we or someone we love are not delivered from danger, disease, injury, or death, we are offended at God. Doubt enters, and we question the Lord's faithfulness, then Scripture verses about his faithfulness, and finally the Bible in general.

If we would read one more verse, we might recognize that Jesus did not promise us a pain-free, accident-free, safe-in-a-bubble existence.

"By your [patient] endurance [empowered by the Holy Spirit] you will gain your souls."[369]

Within the context of the other verses, the promise of protection refers to eternal life, not to physical death or harm. Jesus promises that regardless of physical persecution, even martyrdom, we will suffer no injury that will threaten or jeopardize our salvation.

The Holy Spirit does indeed sometimes deliver us from harm, as he delivered Jesus when the Jews tried to stone him. But in the end, Jesus was crucified. Paul was delivered from stoning.[370] Stephen was not.[371] But despite everything he had suffered for Christ, Paul's sonship, adoption, and salvation were never imperiled.[372]

There's a popular song that says, "when you don't understand, when you don't see his plan, when you can't trace his hand, trust his heart."[373]

We need always to remember that *everything* God does in our lives is motivated by love.

---

[368] Luke 21:12-18, emphasis added.
[369] Ibid., v. 19 AMP.
[370] 2 Corinthians 11:25 NKJV.
[371] Acts 7:59 NKJV.
[372] 2 Timothy 4:7-8.
[373] *Trust His Heart*, Eddie Carswell, Babbie Mason, 1969, Dayspring Music, LLC.

depression

As I write this, depression seems to be pandemic throughout today's cultures. TV commercials and magazine ads hawk treatments like Zoloft, Prozac, Celexa, Lexapro, Paxil, Luvox, Oleptro, and Cymbalta. People everywhere are popping oxidase inhibitors, serotonin and norepinephrine reuptake inhibitors, dopamine reuptake blockers, tricyclic antidepressants, 5-HT2 receptor antagonists, noradrenergic antagonists...or just staring at walls.

And prophets are just as vulnerable, sometimes more so. Remember Elijah under the broom tree? Or Solomon (who you wouldn't think would have a problem with depression, given that he lived in a palace, was paid 25 tons of gold a year,[374] and had 700 wives and 300 concubines.[375]). Yet, we find him whining:

> Smoke, that's what it is. A bad business from start to finish. So what do you get from a life of hard labor? Pain and grief from dawn to dusk. Never a decent night's rest. Nothing but smoke.[376]

despair

Actually, despair is really more of a symptom. Unbelief is the root of the problem, which sets spinning a deadly spiral.

The more unbelief we have, the less realistic our expectations. The more unmet expectations, the more hope deferred, and the greater the discouragement and depression, which leads to more unbelief.

While many physicians prescribe medications to check chemical imbalances of the mind and body, I believe opening a door to unbelief and despair gives the enemy license to manifest it in our DNA and body chemistry. And since the sins of the fathers are visited on the next four generations,[377] despair can legally be passed down to children, grandchildren, and great grandchildren.

---

[374] 2 Chronicles 9:13.
[375] 1 Kings 11:3.
[376] Ecclesiastes 2:22-23 MSG.
[377] Numbers 14:18.

When in doubt, ask the Holy Spirit. He will expose it, if we ask him, and lead us to repentance, thereby closing and locking that door.

Despair and discontent sap not only our mental and physical strength, but also our faith, without which it is impossible to please God. It impairs our intimacy with the Holy Spirit, which is the prophet's source of power and revelation. And it damages our testimony of Jesus, which is the spirit of prophecy. Discontent makes us start to compare ourselves with others who prosper more than we do or get more detailed words of knowledge, whose gifting is more recognized or who are in more demand as speakers.

> So watch your step, friends. Make sure there's no evil unbelief lying around that will trip you up and throw you off course, diverting you from the living God. For as long as it's still God's Today, keep each other on your toes so sin doesn't slow down your reflexes. If we can only keep our grip on the sure thing we started out with, we're in this with Christ for the long haul.[378]

unholy alliances

Scripture speaks of several kinds of unholy alliances. An alliance is a relationship and includes covenants and treaties. It establishes a bond, commitment, or reliance between people. An *unholy* alliance, then, is a relationship that is opposed to, hostile toward, and incompatible with the kingdom of God.

> Woe to those who go down to Egypt for help *And* rely on horses, and trust in chariots because they are many and in horsemen because they are very strong, but they do not look to the Holy One of Israel, nor seek the LORD!...
>
> Now the Egyptians are men and not God, and their horses are flesh and not spirit;

---

[378] Hebrews 3:12 MSG.

so the LORD will stretch out His hand,
and he who helps will stumble and he
who is helped will fall, and all of them
will come to an end together.[379]

This is what the LORD says: "Cursed is
the one who trusts in man, who draws
strength from mere flesh and whose
heart turns away from the LORD."[380]

Jesus said if we're in the world, we're going to have problems.[381]
Sometimes, however, we have a lot more trouble than normal.

I had a season like this and couldn't understand why I was being
hammered from every direction all the time. One day, I asked the
Lord about it when I heard the words, "unholy alliances," and the
Holy Spirit revealed that I had tolerated the spirit of Jezebel in my
life.

I called to Melanie and told her what the Lord had said, and she told
me those were the exact words she had been praying over me. She
said she hadn't told me because I had let people's demands on me
steal my time with the Lord and my family, and I was exhausted and
irritable with those close to me.

Truth be told, people just wanted me for what I could give them
prophetically, and the pressure to perform was killing me. Melanie
said I should inquire of the Lord how to deal with the problem.

At that time, I didn't understand that most prophets battle with
rejection and struggle to hold their lives together. In response, we
can tend to court the acceptance of people, which the Bible calls the
fear of man.

The fear of human opinion disables; trusting in
God protects you from that.[382]

---

[379] Isaiah 31:1, 3 NASB.
[380] Jeremiah 17:5.
[381] John 16:33.
[382] Proverbs 29:25 MSG.

The fear of man opens the gate to create unholy alliances which give the Jezebel spirit legal grounds to destroy the prophet from within.

I repented for tolerating Jezebel in my life and then asked the Lord what I needed to do to recover the boundaries in my life and end the battle raging inside me.

The Lord told me to declare a decree of divorce with Jezebel. I sat down with a tablet and pen, and the Holy Spirit gave me a list of more than one hundred fifty names, including some from my past.

Melanie sat with me, and we declared a decree of divorce over each one of the names and broke all soul ties and words of agreement that were made with them. Then we shared communion and declared that we are bone of Christ's bone and flesh of his flesh and that, outside of our relationship with Jesus and each other, no one had access to us any longer.

That day, I slept for a solid eight hours. It was like heaven.

Afterward, I felt wonderfully light and undistracted. Though no one knew about any of this, I started receiving letters from some of the people on the list, informing me that they were releasing themselves from us and our ministry—confirmation that the soul ties were real and had been broken.

> Do not be yoked together with unbelievers. For what
> do righteousness and wickedness have in common?
> Or what fellowship can light have with
> darkness?[383]

rejection

Rejection is one of the most devastating weapons the enemy uses against God's prophets, because it throws open the door to a mob of familiar spirits including Hate, Jealousy, Envy, Strife, and Murder.

Abel became a shepherd, while Cain was a farmer.

---

[383] 2 Corinthians 6:14.

At harvest time Cain brought the Lord a gift of his farm produce, and Abel brought the fatty cuts of meat from his best lambs, and presented them to the Lord. And the Lord accepted Abel's offering, but not Cain's.

This made Cain both dejected and very angry, and his face grew dark with fury.

"Why are you angry?" the Lord asked him. "Why is your face so dark with rage? It can be bright with joy if you will do what you should! But if you refuse to obey, watch out. Sin is waiting to attack you, longing to destroy you. But you can conquer it!" One day Cain suggested to his brother, "Let's go out into the fields." And while they were together there, Cain attacked and killed his brother.[384]

Cain received the Lord's correction as rejection and took out his outrage on his brother.

Thousands of years—and countless murders—later, God sent his own Son to atone for Abel's murder and for every other sin committed by mankind. And we rejected him.

He came to that which was his own, but his own did not receive him.[385]

He healed sicknesses and diseases and raised the dead to life. And even his family and neighbors rejected him.

But Jesus said to them, "A prophet is not without honor except in his own country, among his own relatives, and in his own house."[386]

And he warned that we, too, will be rejected.

---

[384] Genesis 4:2-8 TLB.
[385] John 1:11.
[386] Mark 6:4 NKJV.

Remember what I told you: 'A servant is not greater than his master.' If they persecuted me, they will persecute you also.[387]

Jesus spoke here of the world. But most of the persecution against God's prophets comes at the hands of God's people.

Jerusalem, Jerusalem, you who kill the prophets and stone those sent to you, how often I have longed to gather your children together, as a hen gathers her chicks under her wings, and you were not willing.[388]

Rejection entered my life right after I was born, taken from my mother and placed in an orphanage.

Growing up, I never experienced any affirmation or relationship, which watered the seeds of rejection, until my garden was overgrown with self-hatred.

I tried everything to get my father's attention. I played rugby at school. Though I was built like a stick figure and too small to play, I fought on the field like someone demonized. But my father never came to a single game.

Because I was rejected by my father, I felt rejected by everyone else.

When I finally realized that I was unacceptable to him, I quit trying and slid deeper into depravity and self-loathing. When I excelled in the military or in business, I never felt good enough, which made me furious at a God I didn't even believe in. I wanted to die.

The root of rejection seared my conscience. My life became a blank canvas on which the enemy of my soul painted its likeness.

You might think that everything changed after I was saved, but the rejection has continued. Now, however, it is at the hands of my brothers and sisters, some of whom reject the prophetic itself while

---

[387] John 15:20.
[388] Luke 13:34.

others reject me personally.

The root of rejection is in the garden of Eden. When Adam and Eve sinned, they were not only cast out of the garden, but also became totally different people. No longer were they people who walked with the Lord. No longer did they have authority over creation. They lost eternal life. They lost the purity of their souls. They now *knew*—experienced, embraced, were intimate with—both good and evil. No longer in right standing with God, their worldview changed radically. They entered a warzone, suddenly engaged in a lifetime struggle with sin and temptation. Essentially, rejection is an identity crisis.

Having spent most of my life under the boot heel of Rejection, I plunged into study and prayer, searching for both a solution and a defense—the former to heal the wounds I had already sustained, the latter to protect myself against future attacks. I spent countless hours praying and asking the Lord for deliverance. And every time, the reply was the same.

"I have given you my Spirit and grace and will not allow you to be tested beyond what you can handle. Speak to Rejection!"

I finally realized it was my problem, not the Lord's, and that I had in hand everything I needed to fix it.

> For His divine power has bestowed on us [absolutely] everything necessary for [a dynamic spiritual] life and godliness, through true *and* personal knowledge of Him who called us by His own glory and excellence.[389]

I wrote myself a daily affirmation of God's truth—my sonship,[390] acceptance[391] and approval. My worthiness as a result of Christ's blood shed for me[392] and the seal of the Holy Spirit upon me.[393] I

---

[389] 2 Peter 1:3 AMP.
[390] Romans 8:17.
[391] Romans 15:7.
[392] Colossians 1:21-22.
[393] Ephesians 1:13.

reminded myself constantly that the grace of God teaches me "to say 'No' to ungodliness and worldly passions, and to live a self-controlled, upright and godly life in this present age."[394] And gradually, the truth of God displaced the rejection and healed my wounds. I learned the powerful truth that I am responsible for my own thoughts[395] and feelings and therefore have control of them. They do not control me.

If our identity is in anything or anyone but Christ, we are targets for rejection. If my identity is in my strength and I grow weak or infirm, who am I? If my identity is in my physical appearance and I grow old or am disfigured, who am I? If my identity is in my calling or my spiritual gift and someone destroys my reputation, who am I? But if my ID card reads: Beloved of God, nothing can change that.

> For I am convinced that neither death nor life, neither angels nor demons, neither the present nor the future, nor any powers, neither height nor depth, nor anything else in all creation, will be able to separate us from the love of God that is in Christ Jesus our Lord.[396]

betrayal

> At that time many will fall away and will betray one another and hate one another. Many false prophets will arise and will mislead many. Because lawlessness is increased, most people's love will grow cold. But the one who endures to the end, he will be saved. This gospel of the kingdom shall be preached in the whole world as a testimony to all the nations, and then the end will come.[397]

Addressing the end times, Jesus said God's children will be betrayed, some even by other believers. He himself was betrayed by

---

[394] Titus 2:12.
[395] 2 Corinthians 10:5.
[396] Romans 8:38-39.
[397] Matthew 24:10-14 NASB.

one of his twelve hand-picked disciples—a man who walked and ate and slept with him day in, day out, for several years, a man Jesus entrusted with his life, as well as his finances. And because a servant is not greater than his master,[398] prophets should not be startled when it happens to us.

I have suffered betrayal many times, mostly from those closest to me. The wounds are so deep that it is hard, even now, to write about it without feeling the pain again.

Betrayal is like being shot. It hits your nervous system like a shockwave and radiates to every part of your body, soul, and spirit.

Prophet Dianne Palmer[399] once sang a prophetic song over me that ministered to the wounds of betrayal in my life.

> And your anointing will increase. You will not shy away like a turtle into your shell anymore. And you said, "The pain of the military was nothing compared to this—when I gave them my best, when I loved them, when I gave them everything for you, God, they turned me away, accused me, abused me, and tried to wound me."
>
> Now I will cause them to stand with you, and they have got your back, man of God. All the abandonment and the pain, but I love you! I love you!

After we came to America, a time came when we couldn't pay the rent, and we received an eviction notice. With three young children and the sudden threat of homelessness, Melanie and I were stressed. We reached out to the people closest to us. One told me he felt I had missed God's timing for immigration to America, and he believed the Lord was forcing us to return to South Africa. Another told me the Lord had given him a red light and we were on our own. This was like getting punched in the gut, since they had all told us in the beginning that the Holy Spirit had sent them to support us. The

---

[398] John 15:20.
[399] https://www.facebook.com/DiannePalmerMinistries.

situation turned from unfaithfulness to betrayal when I learned they had agreed together to withhold help from me and my family.

A few years later, I realized the Lord had used betrayal to sever us from these people for our good. I had become so dependent upon them that the Lord allowed me to be rejected so he could be my help. Even in the midst of betrayal, the Lord brings light out of darkness. Betrayal swept Jesus into his Father's plan of suffering and execution and from that into the blazing light of resurrection.

waiting on the Lord

> He gives strength to the weary, and to him who has no might He increases power. Even youths grow weary and tired, and vigorous young men stumble badly, but those who wait for the Lord [who expect, look for, and hope in Him] will gain new strength *and* renew their power; they will lift up their wings [and rise up close to God] like eagles [rising toward the sun]; they will run and not become weary, they will walk and not grow tired.[400]

Waiting may sound passive, but it may be the most strenuous activity in God's kingdom, particularly when God is silent.

In silent times,
uncertain times,
I wait.
Searching for your face,
stretching to hear your voice,
passionately, eagerly.
Straining.
Restraining.
Frantic to remain still.
Aching to make something happen.
Prodded, goaded by others
to make something happen,

---

[400] Isaiah 40:29-31 AMP.

in the certainty that I must not,
dare not
make something happen.
Waiting.
Hard,
fiery,
furious
waiting.[401]

As a lifestyle, waiting on the Lord is the defining discipline of the prophet. Waiting on the Lord is an ongoing conflict between soul and spirit, "smashing warped philosophies, tearing down barriers erected against the truth of God, fitting every loose thought and emotion and impulse into the structure of life shaped by Christ."[402]

Sometimes, waiting on the Lord is yielding to the Lord's timing.

> For the revelation awaits an appointed time; it speaks of the end and will not prove false. Though it linger, wait for it; it will certainly come and will not delay.[403]

Though the movie *Braveheart* was far from historical, it offers a vivid illustration of the virtue of patience. Until September 11, 1297, the English Light Horse Calvary was undefeated. In the film, William Wallace fashioned hundreds of lances from the trees of the forest and concealed them on the field of battle.

Even after the professional forces of John de Warenne, 6th Earl of Surrey, began their charge, Wallace's men waited. The ground shook beneath the hooves of the English warhorses. Yet, the Scots waited. Finally, when cavalry was so close that it could not disengage, Wallace gave the command, and his men raised the deadly lances, impaling the horses and winning the battle.

I remember ministering in a congregation once when the Holy Spirit

[401] Brackin, Ron, *you and me and the blackthorn tree: verses to the king*, Weller & Bunsby, Publishers, 2011, pp. 118-119, ISBN: 978-0-9897463-7-3.
[402] 2 Corinthians 10:5-6 MSG.
[403] Habakkuk 2:3.

spoke to me about a young girl. I wanted to call her out and share what the Lord was saying, but I felt constrained. When I asked why I wasn't released to speak, the Holy Spirit prompted me just to pray and intercede for her.

Fast forward about three months. I was ministering at the same church. Again the little girl and her mother were there, and this time the Holy Spirit released me to speak.

"Yesterday," I said, "you told your mother, 'Mother, you have no idea what my thoughts are and what my struggles are."

Then I told her that her father would soon face a life-changing experience, and the Lord wanted her to be there to intercede for him.

After the meeting, the girl's mother came up to me and confirmed that those were the exact words her daughter had spoken.

The next time I visited the church, the young lady brought her father to meet me. They told me he had collapsed in the bathroom while the family was away. His daughter, however, was with him.

Remembering the word I had spoken, she began CPR and called 911. While he was in the hospital, the doctors diagnosed a heart problem, which they corrected.

Also, while in the hospital, his daughter played for him the CD with the word I had given, at which time he broke down and cried, and she led him to the Lord. If I had spoken the word to her when I first heard it, the timing would have been wrong and the word would not have made the specific impact that it did. The word of knowledge about her discussion with her mother had convinced her that it was from the Lord and empowered her to function in her redemptive capacity to save her father's natural life and secure his eternal life. Waiting on the Lord always leads to blessing and often to trials.

blessed trials

Maybe the best way to look at trials is the way an athlete looks at pumping iron. It hurts but makes us stronger.

> Consider it pure joy, my brothers and sisters, whenever you face trials of many kinds, because you know that the testing of your faith produces perseverance. Let perseverance finish its work so that you may be mature and complete, not lacking anything.[404]

The joy James refers to does not mean happiness; joy is our assurance of, and security in, Christ's immutable, invariable, incomprehensible love for us. It's the confidence that everything he does in our lives is for our benefit, regardless of how it feels or seems to us at the time. Joy enables us to see far beyond our immediate circumstances, like Jesus "who for the joy set before Him endured the cross, despising the shame."[405]

Trials test God's word in us and validate its truth. Even Jesus benefited from trials.

> Although He was a Son [who had never been disobedient to the Father], He learned [active, special] obedience through what He suffered.[406]

Jesus always knew who he was. For thirty-three years, he worked as a carpenter, waiting for his Father's perfect timing. So the devil tried to thwart God's plan by tempting his Son to reveal himself prematurely. [407]

Being overlooked can test the grit and integrity of the prophet and tempt him to make room for himself—never a good idea.

> For all those who exalt themselves will be humbled, and those who humble themselves will be exalted.[408]

The Holy Spirit has often placed me on the dais with many widely-known men and women of God, where I knew I would be

---

[404] James 1:2-4.
[405] Hebrews 12:2 NASB.
[406] Hebrews 5:8 AMP.
[407] Matthew 4:1-11.
[408] Luke 14:11.

overlooked. At first, it upset me and I tried to think of what I could do to be accepted in what appeared to me at the time the "prophet's clique." Thankfully, the Holy Spirit had instilled in me a greater fear of the Lord than concern for the recognition of men, which overpowered my fleshly desire to be received.

If you are a prophet, you will function as a prophet, regardless of whether or not your prophetic office is recognized. Israel did not recognize its Messiah. Nevertheless, Jesus redeemed them through his atoning death on the cross. Trials purify us, as fire purifies gold, causing the impure dross to float to the top and be skimmed off.

> He knows the way I take; *When* He has tried me,
> I shall come forth as gold.[409]

Trials are opportunities to overcome temptations and challenges and to earn amazing rewards.

> Blessed [happy, spiritually prosperous, favored by God] is the man who is steadfast under trial *and* perseveres when tempted; for when he has passed the test *and* been approved, he will receive the [victor's] crown of life which *the Lord* has promised to those who love Him.[410]

And a crown isn't the only reward. Overcomers get:

- "the right to eat from the tree of life, which is in the paradise of God,[411] he will not be hurt at all by the second death.[412]

- hidden manna and a white stone with a new name written on it, known only to him who receives it.[413]

- authority over the nations and the morning star.[414]

---

[409] Job 23:10 NASB.
[410] James 1:12 AMP.
[411] Revelation 2:7.
[412] Ibid., v. 11.
[413] Ibid., v. 17.
[414] Ibid., vv. 26, 28.

- white clothes, for they are worthy, and God will never blot out their names from the book of life, but will acknowledge their names before the Father and his angels.[415]

- to be a pillar in the temple of God. Never again will he leave it. Jesus will write on him the name of his God and the name of the city of his God, the new Jerusalem, which is coming down out of heaven from his God, and he will also write on him Christ's new name.[416]

- the right to sit with Jesus on his throne just as he overcame and sat down with his Father on his throne.[417]

What does all that mean? I don't know, but I'm guessing that it's greater than any trial, loss, or devastation.

David had a great destiny which brought with it great trials. In one incident alone, he lost the city of Ziklag, his wives and the wives and children of his soldiers were taken captive, and his own people wanted to stone him.[418] Trials often come just when we're getting started. That's because the devil is a baby killer. He tried to kill newborn Moses, newborn Israel, and newborn Jesus. And he's coming after the newborn prophetic ministry as well.

I was rolling along, minding my own business, when the prophetic call and anointing came. Suddenly, my life fell apart. Everything I touched went wrong. My closest friends back in South Africa mocked me and treated me like a leper. Favor slammed the door in my face. I cried out to the Lord. What had I done wrong? But there was no reply. Finally, the Holy Spirit sent a prophet from San Antonio. He spent three days ministering to us about our new calling. He used terms and spoke of concepts I had never heard before that sent me to the Lord to find out what they meant.

The bottom line was that we had stepped out of an ordinary life into an extraordinary life, and all the rules had changed. It was no longer

---

[415] Ibid., 3:4-5.
[416] Ibid., v. 12.
[417] Ibid., v. 21.
[418] 1 Samuel 30:1-6.

business as usual. I had to learn an entirely new way of life that included humbling myself to the Lord and asking for direction every day, like David did against the Amalekite raiding party that took his wives.

> Then…David inquired of the LORD, "Shall I pursue this raiding party? Will I overtake them?"
>
> "Pursue them," he answered. "You will certainly overtake them and succeed in the rescue."[419]

So I chose the path of most resistance. I prayed and waited on the Lord for vindication…which took a very, very long time.

Trials expose the strengths and weaknesses of our foundation.

> "Why are you so polite with me, always saying 'Yes, sir,' and 'That's right, sir,' but never doing a thing I tell you? These words I speak to you are not mere additions to your life, homeowner improvements to your standard of living. They are foundation words, words to build a life on. "If you work the words into your life, you are like a smart carpenter who dug deep and laid the foundation of his house on bedrock. When the river burst its banks and crashed against the house, nothing could shake it; it was built to last. But if you just use my words in Bible studies and don't work them into your life, you are like a dumb carpenter who built a house but skipped the foundation. When the swollen river came crashing in, it collapsed like a house of cards. It was a total loss."[420]

Trials establish us.

> You're not the only ones plunged into these hard times. It's the same with Christians all over the

---

419 Ibid., 7-8.
420 Luke 6:46-49 MSG.

world. So keep a firm grip on the faith. The suffering won't last forever. It won't be long before this generous God who has great plans for us in Christ—eternal and glorious plans they are! —will have you put together and on your feet for good. He gets the last word; yes, he does.[421]

Maybe the best news about trials is that we will never go through them alone. Though no one else stands with us, though no one even understands what we're suffering, the Holy Spirit is with us and understands perfectly.

I am with you and will watch over you wherever you go, and I will bring you back to this land. I will not leave you until I have done what I have promised you." When Jacob awoke from his sleep, he thought, "Surely the LORD is in this place, and I was not aware of it."[422]

Trust God, devote yourself to prayer, keep the faith, rest in the Lord.

So we're not giving up. How could we! Even though on the outside it often looks like things are falling apart on us, on the inside, where God is making new life, not a day goes by without his unfolding grace.

These hard times are small potatoes compared to the coming good times, the lavish celebration prepared for us. There's far more here than meets the eye. The things we see now are here today, gone tomorrow. But the things we can't see now will last forever.[423]

When all is said and done, rejoice! Learn to embrace your trials, for they are the chisel in God's hand that chips away at everything that is not Jesus, until you are transformed into his likeness.

---

[421] 1 Peter 5:9-10 MSG.
[422] Genesis 28:15-16.
[423] 2 Corinthians 4:17-18 MSG.

If you allow them to, your trials will even leave behind blessings for others.

You can only repeat what you've been taught, but you can impart what God has wrought in you.

CHAPTER TEN
the prophet in the congregation(s)

> When people ask me to describe the prophetic ministry, I
> tell them it's like an Oreo cookie. One chocolate wafer is
> the will of God, the other chocolate wafer is the desire of
> the people, and the prophet is the white stuff squished
> between them.
>
> ~ Ron Campbell

Agabus, believed by historians to be one of the seventy
disciples,[424] is the first New Testament prophet mentioned
in Scripture. [425]

> During this time some prophets came down from
> Jerusalem to Antioch. One of them, named
> Agabus, stood up and through the Spirit predicted
> that a severe famine would spread over the entire
> Roman world. (This happened during the reign of
> Claudius.) The disciples, as each one was able,
> decided to provide help for the brothers and sisters
> living in Judea. This they did, sending their gift to
> the elders by Barnabas and Saul.[426]

So the first thing we see about the prophetic in the congregation(s)

---

[424] Luke 10:1 NASB.

[425] Though many think of John the Baptist as a New Testament prophet, he was actually
the last and greatest (Matthew 11:11) prophet under the Old Covenant. The New Covenant
began with the death and resurrection of Jesus, who himself declared that "whoever is least
in the kingdom of heaven is greater than [John the Baptist]."

[426] Acts 11:27-30, Ironically, the name Agabus means *locust*. At the peak of the famine
(46-47 A.D.), the Jerusalem Christians depended on help from their brothers and sisters in
Antioch (Antakya, Turkey), while the Jews in Jerusalem received relief from Helena, queen
of Adiabene (Irbil, Iraq), who had recently converted to Judaism and bought grain from
Egypt.

is that prophets are sometimes sent by their home churches to bless other churches. Agabus was sent by Jerusalem to Antioch. Saul and Barnabas were sent by Antioch to Jerusalem.

Sometime later, Saul and Barnabas were sent out again.

> Now in the church at Antioch there were prophets and teachers: Barnabas, Simeon called Niger, Lucius of Cyrene, Manaen (who had been brought up with Herod the tetrarch) and Saul. While they were worshiping the Lord and fasting, the Holy Spirit said, "Set apart for me Barnabas and Saul for the work to which I have called them." So after they had fasted and prayed, they placed their hands on them and sent them off.[427]

At least five prophets—Barnabas, Simeon, Lucius, Manaen, and Saul—ministered in the Antioch church. Two were sent from there by the Holy Spirit to carry the gospel of the kingdom of God throughout Cyprus and Turkey, "strengthening the disciples and encouraging them to remain true to the faith," appointing elders in each church, and committing them to the Lord.[428]

Another time, when Judaizers went down to Antioch preaching circumcision, the Jerusalem church sent two more of their prophets—Judas and Silas—to accompany Saul and Barnabas with a letter to the Gentile believers in Antioch, telling them they did not have to follow Jewish tradition in order to follow Christ.

During their stay in Antioch, Judas and Silas "said much to encourage and strengthen the believers. After spending some time there, they were sent off by the believers with the blessing of peace to return to those who had sent them. But Paul and Barnabas remained in Antioch, where they and many others taught and preached the word of the Lord."[429]

The prophet Agabus appears once again in Caesarea, where he "took

---

[427] Acts 13:1-3.
[428] Acts 14:22-23.
[429] Acts 15:32-35.

Paul's belt, tied his own hands and feet with it and said, 'The Holy Spirit says, "In this way the Jewish leaders in Jerusalem will bind the owner of this belt and will hand him over to the Gentiles."'"[430]

While not a comprehensive job description of New Testament prophets in the congregation, the Bible tells us that they:

- reside in a home congregation
- serve as emissaries
- minister prophetically to church leaders
- minister prophetically in other congregations
- carry the gospel of the kingdom of God to the lost
- strengthen and encourage the brethren
- preach and teach the word of the Lord
- anoint elders in the churches and commit them to the Lord

prophetic ministry to the congregation

Personal prophecy is much more than an announcement or declaration of a future event or revelation of God's destiny for us. It carries the power to become. The first prophetic utterance is recorded in Genesis 1:3:

> And God said, "Let there be light," and there was light.

In the same way, Jesus prophetically declared his Father's will to demons and infirmities, and it was so. And he imparted that power to us.

> Truly I say to you, whoever says to this mountain,
> 'Be taken up and cast into the sea,' and does not
> doubt in his heart, but believes that what he says
> is going to happen, it will be *granted* him.[431]

Prophecy also carries the power to transform.

When Israel rejected God and demanded a king like other nations,

---

[430] Acts 21:10-11.
[431] Mark 11:23 NASB.

God selected a man named Saul from the least of the clans of the smallest tribe of Israel to rule over them. Then he revealed his choice to his prophet, Samuel.

> About this time tomorrow I will send you a man from the land of Benjamin. Anoint him ruler over my people Israel; he will deliver them from the hand of the Philistines. [432]

Saul was tall and good looking, but that was about all he had going for him. When the Lord chose him, Saul was out searching for his father's lost donkeys. One day, his servant suggested that they go to Ramah, where the prophet was known to be.

Instead of telling him where his father's donkeys were, however, Samuel shocked Saul by inviting him to dinner and seating him at the place of honor. The next day, Samuel took Saul aside, poured olive oil on his head, kissed him, and said, "Has not the Lord anointed you ruler over his inheritance?"

Then Samuel prophesied over him.

> When you leave me today, you will meet two men near Rachel's tomb, at Zelzah on the border of Benjamin. They will say to you, 'The donkeys you set out to look for have been found. And now your father has stopped thinking about them and is worried about you. He is asking, "What shall I do about my son?"' Then you will go on from there until you reach the great tree of Tabor. Three men going up to worship God at Bethel will meet you there. One will be carrying three young goats, another three loaves of bread, and another a skin of wine. They will greet you and offer you two loaves of bread, which you will accept from them. [433]

This prophetic sign was a powerful confirmation of Saul's royal

---

[432] 1 Samuel 9:15-16.
[433] Ibid., 10:2-4.

180

anointing. The bread was being taken to the house of the Lord as an offering. By presenting Saul with two of the loaves, the men acknowledged that the gifts were his due as their king.

A second, life-changing confirmation was to follow.

> After that you will go to Gibeah of God, where there is a Philistine outpost. As you approach the town, you will meet a procession of prophets coming down from the high place with lyres, timbrels, pipes and harps being played before them, and they will be prophesying. The Spirit of the LORD will come powerfully upon you, and you will prophesy with them; *and you will be changed into a different person.*[434]

As Saul followed Samuel's instructions, the Holy Spirit began to transform him from a donkey-chaser into a king, into God's predetermined reality. When we follow a prophet's instructions, God honors us by backing up his word.

> Once these signs are fulfilled, do whatever your hand finds to do, for God is with you.[435]

To best respond to a prophetic word, however, we need to sow seeds of faith and thanksgiving into its fulfillment.

> Go down ahead of me to Gilgal. I will surely come down to you to sacrifice burnt offerings and fellowship offerings, but you must wait seven days until I come to you and tell you what you are to do.[436]

The word began to become reality as soon as Saul took his first step of obedience.

> As Saul turned to leave Samuel, God changed

---

[434] Verses 5-6, emphasis added.
[435] Verse 7.
[436] Verse 8.

Saul's heart, and all these signs were fulfilled that day.[437]

Saul, for all his subsequent weaknesses and faults, received the prophet's words as the words of God and acted on them.

When I first set out on my prophetic path, I didn't understand these principles. Back then I cherry picked prophetic words. I agreed with the parts I liked, and if there was a part I didn't like or understand, I told myself the prophet must have missed God, giving myself a back door so I didn't have to feel responsible for the entire word. I even finessed Scripture to prove my position. First Corinthians 13:9 provided a particularly effective excuse.

For we know in part and we prophesy in part...

So I took prophecies a-part.

One time, I ignored a prophetic word because it didn't seem to fit my existing circumstances. I wasn't "rightly dividing the word"[438] or taking it to the Lord in prayer or coming into agreement with it.

Imagine my surprise when the very thing I disagreed with happened exactly as the prophet said it would, exactly when he said it would happen. It turned out to be a tremendous blessing, and I was humbled that the Holy Spirit had fulfilled the word in spite of my arrogance.

Instead of dissecting God's prophetic words, we need to turn them into prayers.

Today, when a word is spoken over me, I write it out and color-code it, highlighting promises in blue marker. Then I write down any Scripture verses the Holy Spirit puts in my heart and declare both the word and the verses until I see the word fulfilled.

I've also learned that it's very important to keep my eyes on the Lord's promise and not on the result I expect.

---

[437] Verse 9.
[438] 2 Timothy 2:15 NKJV.

Recalling again my formative years, whenever the Lord said he was going to pour out a financial blessing and I started to "pray it in," I found myself looking at the prosperity of people around me and wondering why it seemed to elude me.

I talked to Andrew about it, and he explained that I was falling into Cain's trap, the one that ended with fratricide. Andrew called it the "delusion of comparing." I thought personal prosperity was confirmation that someone was in the Lord's will. It was a subtle shift from praying the promise to praying the result. The former is an act of faith; the latter is manipulation.

prophets must be accountable

Prophets often tend to be loners, which can be dangerous.

> A man who isolates himself seeks his own desire;
> he rages against all wise judgment.[439]

This is why the prophet needs to be accountable to local church leaders who the Lord often uses to save the prophet from himself.

Like apostles, prophets are hardwired and impassioned to build. And because they see God's plans, it's natural for them to want to get in there and do it themselves rather than to let others roll up their sleeves and go to work. But prophets who give in to this temptation can find themselves interfering with the Lord.

A few years ago, I was privileged to spend time at the home of a wealthy businessman and his family. As the weekend progressed, I shared a little about my personal prophetic path, prayed over their marriage and children, and told them about the grace that had been assigned to them by the Lord. The Lord's presence and peace were palpable the entire time.

One Sunday evening, the businessman took me into his library.

Opening his checkbook, he asked, "What are you building?"

---

[439] Proverbs 18:1 NKJV.

I was still thinking about all the things I had in mind to do for the Lord when I heard myself reply, "Absolutely nothing."

I was shocked! What had come out of my mouth certainly had not originated in my head.

"That's the strangest thing I have ever heard!" he said, closing the checkbook. And reeling with regret and anger, I went to my room that night to talk to the Lord.

"Why not me!"

"The first time men tried to build something for their own glory," the Holy Spirit said, "I confused their language."[440]

"Oh," I said, gently chastised.

When people try to build ministries—or the church—apart from the Holy Spirit's initiation and involvement, the inevitable result is confusion and discord.

"*I* will build my church," the Lord told Peter, "and the gates of Hades will not overcome it."[441]

The Lord protected me from my own zeal as I yielded to his.

> Of the greatness of his government and peace there will be no end. He will reign on David's throne and over his kingdom, establishing and upholding it with justice and righteousness from that time on and forever. *The zeal of the LORD Almighty will accomplish this.*[442]

prophetic ministry to church leaders

Just as members of a congregation need the benefit of prophets, so do their leaders.

---

[440] Genesis 11:1-9.
[441] Matthew 16:18, emphasis added.
[442] Isaiah 9:7, emphasis added.

I was asked to attend a meeting once where the apostolic authorities over a particular community were trying to resolve a conflict between a pastor and one of his leaders. Failure could lead to a church split and serious collateral damage.

The leader claimed to be able to discern spirits and accused the pastor of operating in a demonic spirit. He demanded that the pastor step down and insisted that he take over until the pastor could be restored. The discussion was going nowhere quickly, with everyone just giving opinions.

At one point, one of the apostolic leaders looked over at me and said, "You're being very quiet. Aren't you going to say something?"

"I wasn't invited in to say anything, so I just held my peace."

"We value your opinion, so speak."

"I don't have an opinion," I told them, "but I do have the word of the Lord."

"Okay," they said, "let's hear it."

"We're dealing with an accusation here, and I heard the Lord say, 'The way to end this stalemate is to use Solomon's principle.'"

I asked both gentlemen if they would submit to a small test and they agreed. The leader who had made the accusation prided himself on his ability to minister deliverance to anyone who was oppressed. I asked the pastor if he would allow this man to bind the demonic spirit, if there was one, and cast it out. He eagerly agreed.

Turning to the leader, I said, "If, in ten minutes, you don't get the enemy dealt with, it's your turn."

The apostolic team looked at me as if I had ridden in on E.T.'s bicycle.

The leader went at it hammer and tongs, shouting and binding and praying in tongues. Ten minutes later, nothing had happened.

I stood up and asked the leader if I could pray for him, and he agreed. As I prayed, the Holy Spirit showed me that he had picked up a spirit of divination in his younger days when he spent time with Wiccans.[443]

Twenty minutes later, the conflict was resolved, the two men were reconciled, and a church split was averted as a result of a direct word from the Lord, instead of personal opinions and fruitless discussion.

restoring the fallen

This brings up the issue of restoring those who have failed.

> Brothers, if anyone is caught in any sin, you who are spiritual [that is, you who are responsive to the guidance of the Spirit] are to restore such a person in a spirit of gentleness [not with a sense of superiority or self-righteousness], keeping a watchful eye on yourself, so that you are not tempted as well.[444]

Nobody ever failed like Peter, who for three years had shared Jesus' most intimate and profound moments. Peter, to whom the Father personally revealed the identity of his Son.[445] Peter, who when things got rough, denied his dearest friend, not once, but three times. Yet, Jesus restored Peter, freely and fully.

> When they had finished eating, Jesus said to Simon Peter, "Simon son of John, do you love me more than these?"
>
> "Yes, Lord," he said, "you know that I love you."
>
> Jesus said, "Feed my lambs."
>
> Again Jesus said, "Simon son of John, do you love me?"

---

[443] A religious movement of neo-pagan witchcraft, begun in England in the 1950s.
[444] Galatians 6:1 AMP.
[445] Matthew 16:13-17.

He answered, "Yes, Lord, you know that I love you."

Jesus said, "Take care of my sheep."

The third time he said to him, "Simon son of John, do you love me?"

Peter was hurt because Jesus asked him the third time, "Do you love me?" He said, "Lord, you know all things; you know that I love you."

Jesus said, "Feed my sheep.[446]

Jesus did not make Peter jump through religious hoops in order to be restored. Peter wasn't disgraced or rejected. No one told him he would never again be able to minister or serve in leadership.

Sadly, this is how we often treat our wounded in the church today.

The Afrikaner high school I attended was like a military academy. Failing a subject, fighting on the playground, tardiness, unexcused absence, wearing your uniform improperly, or any one of a dozen other infractions got you a seat outside the principal's office.

Exposed for everyone to see, you endured the "wait of shame," inevitably followed by the "board of education" being applied energetically and repeatedly to your "seat of learning." No excuses. No grace.

Once you had received three or four cuts with the cane, however, it was over. You were free to return to class. Life moved on. No more embarrassment, shame, or shunning.

wolves in the sheepfold

Another function of the prophetic within the congregation is to protect believers from false prophets.

---

[446] John 21:15-17.

For false messiahs and false prophets will appear and perform signs and wonders to deceive, if possible, even the elect. So be on your guard; I have told you everything ahead of time.[447]

Because "even the elect" can be deceived, God gave prophets to the church who are "bred" to sniff out danger like livestock-guarding dogs in a meadow.

Livestock-guarding dogs, unlike sheepdogs that are bred for herding, are bred specifically to protect the flock. They are introduced into the flock when they're just a few weeks old and live, day in and day out, with the sheep.

By the time they become adults, they know the sheep so well that anything that doesn't smell familiar, sound familiar, or move in a familiar way is identified as a potential enemy.

In Namibia, for example, the Turkish Kangal dog is used to help protect livestock from cheetah attacks. Mostly, however, it watches over flocks.

When suspicious of an intruder, it "will stand with its tail and ears erect and give an alarm call, inciting the sheep to gather around it for protection."[448]

> Watch out for false prophets. They come to you in sheep's clothing, but inwardly they are ferocious wolves.[449]

False prophets have been with us for millennia.

> God's Message came to me: "Son of man, preach against the prophets of Israel who are making things up out of their own heads and calling it 'prophesying.' "Preach to them the real thing. Tell them, 'Listen to *God's* Message!' God, the

---

[447] Mark 13:22-23.
[448] http://www.vontassenfarm.com/Kangal-dogs, retrieved August 9, 2016.
[449] Matthew 7:15.

Master, pronounces doom on the empty-headed prophets who do their own thing and know nothing of what's going on! Your prophets, Israel, are like jackals scavenging through the ruins. They haven't lifted a finger to repair the defenses of the city and have risked nothing to help Israel stand on God's Day of Judgment. All they do is fantasize comforting illusions and preach lying sermons. They say 'God says...' when God hasn't so much as breathed in their direction. And yet they stand around thinking that something they said is going to happen. "Haven't you fantasized sheer nonsense? Aren't your sermons tissues of lies, saying 'God says...' when I've done nothing of the kind? Therefore—and this is the Message of God, the Master, remember—I'm dead set against prophets who substitute illusions for visions and use sermons to tell lies. I'm going to ban them from the council of my people, remove them from membership in Israel, and outlaw them from the land of Israel. Then you'll realize that I am God, the Master.[450]

But the threat of false prophets is particularly virulent today as a result of all the forms of social media available to the saints. Every time the Lord speaks, false voices flood the Internet with declarations that some deep truth was recently revealed to them in a dream or vision.

And as the Lord continues to restore specific gifts to the body of Christ to enable it to mature, the enemy continues to release a cacophony of counterfeits to confuse God's children.

The devil has been very successful, for example, in his strategy to use false prophetic voices to lure Christians away from Christ by getting them to focus on end-time speculation. Many have claimed to foretell the end of time, but no one holds them to account when their word proves to be wrong.

---

[450] Ezekiel 13:1-9 MSG.

One of the most notorious examples was the book, *88 Reasons Why the Rapture Will Be in 1988*, by former NASA engineer and Bible student Edgar C. Whisenant. Three hundred thousand copies of this book were mailed free of charge to ministers across America, and 4.5 million copies were sold.

"Only if the Bible is in error," Whisenant boasted, "am I wrong, and I say that unequivocally."[451]

Whisenant was wrong. And I say that unequivocally.

A friend of mine told me of a young member of his church who, hearing from a false prophet that Jesus would return on such-and-such a date and being advised of the signs that would precede his return, despaired when the date arrived and he had witnessed none of the signs. Believing that God had forsaken him, he bought a handgun and killed himself.

These are just a couple of instances. The Y2K prophecies are another.

The Spirit of Nationalism that we talked about in the previous chapter is one of the biggest recruiters of false prophets among those we esteem to be "in the know."

In election years, they pour out of the woodwork. Some prophesy a victory for this candidate, others for that one. This one, they say, will heal America. No, others insist, our candidate will heal America.

But God does not use his prophets to foretell election outcomes any more than to predict race results. And no man or woman has the power to heal America. Apparently, the false prophets haven't noticed that the Messiah has already come.

Once a group invited me to keep vigil with them over a prophetic word they had received about an election. They were fasting and praying in shifts around the clock to bring the word to pass.

---

[451] Bahnsen, Greg Ph.D., "If You Received This, the World Did Not End," *Penpoint*, Volume V:9, October 1994, Covenant Media Foundation.

I declined their invitation, explaining that the Holy Spirit had not led me to do that, that he had called me to advance the kingdom of God, not the District of Columbia.

When their candidate lost, they accused his opponent of stealing the election, inasmuch as they had the word of the Lord. They even called me and asked what happened. All I could say was that God's ways are higher than ours and no amount of prophecy, prayer, or fasting is going to manipulate the Holy Spirit. They called me a soft-hearted liberal, and I never heard from them again. While voting is our civil privilege, prayer for our elected officials is our responsibility before God.

> First of all, then, I urge that petitions (specific requests), prayers, intercessions (prayers for others) and thanksgivings be offered on behalf of all people, for kings and all who are in [positions of] high authority, so that we may live a peaceful and quiet life in all godliness and dignity. This [kind of praying] is good and acceptable *and* pleasing in the sight of God our Savior...[452]

When a self-proclaimed prophetic voice—in the mail, on the Internet, or from the pulpit—curses, denigrates, dishonors, or threatens candidates or elected officials, imparting fear or hatred, that prophetic voice is *always* false. No exceptions.

> Pay your taxes, pay your bills, respect your leaders.[453]

Because of false prophets, many Christians remain "children [spiritually immature], tossed back and forth [like ships on a stormy sea] and carried about by every wind of [shifting] doctrine, by the cunning *and* trickery of [unscrupulous] men, by the deceitful scheming of people ready to do anything [for personal profit].[454]

Where are the true New Testament prophets today?

---

[452] 1 Timothy 2:1-3 AMP.
[453] Romans 13:7 MSG.
[454] Ephesians 4:14 AMP.

CHAPTER ELEVEN
the prophet in the workplace

> If the goals of marketplace ministry are realized, a new breed of Christianity is in the making—the kind that will change the spiritual climate of the 21st century marketplace, conduct business in the power of the Holy Spirit and generate tremendous financial resources for kingdom purposes.[455]
>
> ~ *Charisma* Magazine

Jesus commissioned us to "Go into all the world and preach the gospel to all creation."[456]

Elementary, right?

So what does the "world" include? Is government part of the world? Entertainment? Education?

What about the workplace?

The fact is that the church, which includes all Christians, is already in every corner and aspect of the world, every day of every week—24-7-365 (or 366, every four years or so).

C. Peter Wagner refers to Christians meeting together on Sundays as the *nuclear church*. All the rest of the time, he says, we're the *extended church*. But nuclear or extended, you and I are the church, no matter where we are or what we're doing—whether in a classroom, showroom, or boardroom, on an assembly line or in line

---

[455] Walker, Ken, "It's Time for Marketplace Ministry, *Charisma Magazine*, May 31, 2003, retrieved from http://www.charismamag.com/site-archives/120-features/unorganized/943-its-time-for-marketplace-ministry, 06-11-16.
[456] Mark 16:15.

at the ballpark. The world is where we grow the fruit of the Holy Spirit and where he intends for us to exercise his gifts.

Prophets should function fully in every part in the world, just as they do in the religious part. But what does the prophetic look like in the workplace?

Unfortunately most people today, when they hear the word prophet, think fortune-teller, albeit a godly fortune-teller. If you doubt that, try to find a parking space when a prophet comes to town. Let's face it, prophets pack the pews because people want to know their future, not because they want to hear the present word of the Lord.

So when you put the words *prophet* and *workplace* together, people think supernatural insider trading. They imagine prophets selling their Spirit-given gifts for filthy lucre, and the story of Balaam springs to mind.[457]

But the Holy Spirit is restoring the prophetic office to the workplace, just as in the church and in every other part of the world.

For centuries the consensus was that the work of the ministry was confined to the church. In recent years, however, unbiblical concepts of clergy and laity have begun to dissolve as Christians realize that we are all ministers of the gospel—inside and outside the walls of our church buildings. It's who we *are*, it's not what we *do*.

The prophetic, as we have seen, is about transformation, individually and corporately, into the likeness of Jesus Christ. Transforming the body of Christ into his bride. And transforming the kingdoms of this world into the kingdom of our God. Is any aspect of the world in more need of transformation than the workplace?

Throughout the Old Testament, prophets influenced the workplace when they ministered to kings and queens, who were the movers and shakers of commerce and industry, who decreed laws and punished wrongdoers, declared war and sued for peace.

---

[457] Numbers 22-23.

Joseph was the first workplace prophet.

> So Pharaoh said to his servants, "Can we find a man like this [a man equal to Joseph], in whom is the divine spirit [of God]?"[458]

First, he governed the house and property of Potiphar.

> Potiphar put him in charge of his household, and he entrusted to his care everything he owned. From the time he put him in charge of his household and of all that he owned, the LORD blessed the household of the Egyptian because of Joseph. The blessing of the LORD was on everything Potiphar had, both in the house and in the field.[459]

Then he governed all of Egypt.

> So Pharaoh said to Joseph, "I hereby put you in charge of the whole land of Egypt." Then Pharaoh took his signet ring from his finger and put it on Joseph's finger. He dressed him in robes of fine linen and put a gold chain around his neck. He had him ride in a chariot as his second-in-command, and people shouted before him, "Make way!" Thus he put him in charge of the whole land of Egypt.

> Then Pharaoh said to Joseph, "I am Pharaoh, but without your word no one will lift hand or foot in all Egypt." Pharaoh gave Joseph the name Zaphenath-Paneah and gave him Asenath daughter of Potiphera, priest of On, to be his wife. And Joseph went throughout the land of Egypt. Joseph was thirty years old when he entered the service of Pharaoh king of Egypt. And Joseph went out from Pharaoh's presence and traveled

---

[458] Genesis 41:38 AMP.
[459] Genesis 39:4-5.

throughout Egypt. During the seven years of abundance the land produced plentifully. Joseph collected all the food produced in those seven years of abundance in Egypt and stored it in the cities. In each city he put the food grown in the fields surrounding it.

Joseph stored up huge quantities of grain, like the sand of the sea; it was so much that he stopped keeping records because it was beyond measure.[460]

The prophet Moses began as a prince of Egypt, "educated in all the learning of the Egyptians, and he was a man of power in words and deeds."[461] It is difficult to imagine such a man without influence in the workplace and affairs of state.

Other workplace prophets include Samuel, who anointed and advised King Saul and King David; Nathan, who advised David and anointed and advised King Solomon; and Elijah, who advised King Ahab, impacted the nation's religious system,[462] and affected its agricultural industry.[463]

In the New Testament, Prophet Jesus led the way into the workplace when he invaded the life of a crooked civil servant.

Jesus entered Jericho and was passing through. A man was there by the name of Zacchaeus; he was a chief tax collector and was wealthy. He wanted to see who Jesus was, but because he was short he could not see over the crowd. So he ran ahead and climbed a sycamore-fig tree to see him, since Jesus was coming that way.

When Jesus reached the spot, he looked up and said to him, "Zacchaeus, come down immediately. I must

---

[460] Genesis 41:41-49.
[461] Acts 7:22 NAS".
[462] 1 Kings 18:16-40.
[463] 1 Kings 17.

stay at your house today." So he came down at once and welcomed him gladly.[464]

Jesus had eyes to recognize a heart that was ready for the kingdom, whereas everyone else saw only a sleazy businessman.

> All the people saw this and began to mutter, "He has gone to be the guest of a sinner."

Breaking bread is one of the most intimate social activities in Middle Eastern culture. The Jews considered Jesus sitting down to dinner with Zacchaeus to be a notch below blasphemy. If nothing else, it certainly would have caused them to question his spiritual authority.

Though we have no record of the dialogue between Jesus and Zacchaeus, everyone witnessed the results.

> But Zacchaeus stood up and said to the Lord, "Look, Lord! Here and now I give half of my possessions to the poor, and if I have cheated anybody out of anything, I will pay back four times the amount."

Not only did Zacchaeus repent, he also went far above and beyond the requirements of the law.

> The Lord said to Moses, "Say to the Israelites: 'Any man or woman who wrongs another in any way and so is unfaithful to the Lord is guilty and must confess the sin they have committed. They must make full restitution for the wrong they have done, add a fifth of the value to it and give it all to the person they have wronged.

To comply with the law, Zacchaeus would have needed to pay a twenty-percent penalty. Instead, he repaid four hundred percent what he had stolen!

> Jesus said to him, "Today salvation has come to

---

[464] Luke 19:1-6.

this house, because this man, too, is a son of Abraham. For the Son of Man came to seek and to save the lost."

So what does the New Testament prophet look like in the workplace? Frankly, we don't know. We're at the very beginning of restoring the prophetic, both to the church and to the rest of the world. I can only share my own experiences as a glimpse of what might be ahead.

Over the years, I have found a number of principles that I believe apply to prophets in the workplace.

The prophet must remain kingdom-minded. The overriding, intentional, constant objective of the prophet's activities in the workplace is to expand God's kingdom as the Spirit leads.

The seventh angel sounded his trumpet, and there were loud voices in heaven, which said: "The kingdom of the world has become the kingdom of our Lord and of his Messiah, and he will reign for ever and ever."[465]

The kingdoms of this world, including those of labor and commerce, are circumscribed within the kingdom of God. Think fundamental set theory—you know, those circles-intersecting-circles thingies you had to study in school. All the kingdoms of the world are little circles inside the big circle, which is God's kingdom.

For to us a child is born, to us a son is given, and the government will be on his shoulders. And he will be called Wonderful Counselor, Mighty God, Everlasting Father, Prince of Peace.[466]

God might as well have added "President and CEO."

To be truly and eternally successful in the workplace one must first be successful in the kingdom of God. And the only way to do that is

---

[465] Revelation 11:15.
[466] Isaiah 9:6.

to acknowledge the Holy Spirit as Chief Executive Officer and follow his lead.

A company or organization can grow to be very successful by worldly standards, yet be an abject failure in God's kingdom because it failed to fulfill God's purposes.

Likewise a company or organization can appear to have failed miserably in the eyes of the world and Wall Street, yet be a ticker-tape success in the kingdom of God because it did what the Holy Spirit led it to do. If the prophet allows himself to think in terms of profits and paychecks, he will lose sight of his objective and fail himself, his client or employer, and the Lord.

The prophet needs to think generationally, rather than short term, developing and maintaining a long-range perspective in the workplace, and considering how his actions and choices will affect subsequent generations.

Everything Abraham did affected Isaac, everything Isaac did affected Jacob, and everything Jacob did affected Israel. Every choice matters, whether in a cubicle or a corner office on the twenty-sixth floor. The prophet needs to discern the legacy God has destined for the company or organization he serves, then declare it, nurture it, and protect it.

The prophet needs to function redemptively. To redeem, among other things, means to save from error or evil. In the workplace, the prophet influences the lives of decision makers who, in turn, affect everything and everyone under their authority.

> I urge, then, first of all, that petitions, prayers, intercession and thanksgiving be made for all people—for kings and all those in authority, that we may live peaceful and quiet lives in all godliness and holiness.[467]

The prophet must always remember that wealth is a tool, not a goal.

---

[467] 1 Timothy 2:1-3.

Capitalist economies have created a culture of open-ended increase. We have been taught that every year should yield more business and greater dividends, which forces up prices, which forces up wages, which stokes the demand for more business and greater dividends. This can be a dangerous temptation for the prophet, who has the innate ability to release strategy and prophetic anointing to empower the workplace with financial success.

> But remember the Lord your God, for it is he who gives you the ability to produce wealth, and so confirms his covenant, which he swore to your ancestors, as it is today.[468]

Wealth, as a goal, can never be attained. No amount will ever be enough. Wealth, as a tool, helps to accomplish goals. God's kingdom is the goal.

> No one can serve two masters. Either you will hate the one and love the other, or you will be devoted to the one and despise the other. You cannot serve both God and money.[469]

> But seek first his kingdom and his righteousness, and all these things will be given to you as well.[470]

The prophet works to replace a corporate culture with a kingdom culture. In a corporate culture, rewards are lavished on the C-level officials: CEO, CFO, COO, etc. The prophet helps executives understand what Scripture means when it says, "Do not muzzle an ox while it is treading out the grain," and "The worker deserves his wages."[471]

The prophet is called to the workplace to serve.

Corporate executives often treat a prophet with more honor and respect than he receives in his own congregation, which can be

---

[468] Deuteronomy 8:18.
[469] Matthew 6:24.
[470] Matthew 6:33.
[471] 1 Timothy 5:18.

seductive after suffering rejection and betrayals. An inviolable principle of God's kingdom is that the last shall be first and the first last.

"The greatest," Jesus explained, "will be your servant. For those who exalt themselves will be humbled, and those who humble themselves will be exalted."[472] And again, "the Son of Man did not come to be served, but to serve, and to give his life as a ransom for many."[473]

Service yields success, as we saw with Joseph in Potiphar's house and in the house of Pharaoh.

Finally, the workplace needs the entire five-fold ministry.

The Chief Executive Officer (CEO) corresponds loosely to the apostle, the foundation of the workplace. The evangelist is like the Chief Marketing Officer (CMO), who draws people into the economy of God's workplace and carries the responsibility of communicating vision and mission. The pastor is like the Chief Human Resources Officer (CHRO), responsible for daily operations and relationship building in the workplace. The teacher is the Chief Operations Officer (COO), who keeps the message aligned with the mission and is responsible for all workplace operations.

And the prophet corresponds to the Chief Strategic Officer (CSO), also part of the foundation who, in partnership with the CEO, seeks revelation and strategic intuition.

> Chief strategy officer is a consultative role; part leader and part doer with the responsibility of ensuring that execution supports the strategy elements. This unique background takes a multitude of different operating experiences [and] must include being both a creative thinker and influential collaborator.[474]

---

[472] Matthew 23:11-12.
[473] Matthew 20:28.
[474] "The Role of the Chief Strategy Officer, Ephor Group, Retrieved September 14, 2016 from http://www.ephorgroup.com/chiefstrategyofficer.aspisaiah.

The five-fold ministry does not have a switch that automatically activates and deactivates as we walk in and out of the church building. The five-fold ministry functions everywhere we go, just as our faith and our body function everywhere, at all times. There is, however, a growth process. I didn't just wake up one morning, look in the mirror, and see a workplace prophet looking back at me. It was a gradual transition that began on September 10, 2001, when the Holy Spirit told me to liquidate my share portfolio.

So I called my broker and told him to sell everything.

He thought I was crazy. Microsoft was about to split, he argued, and I would earn a great yield.

"No," I insisted, "sell everything."

The next morning, terrorists destroyed the World Trade Center. The stock market shut down, and shares dropped through the floor. In addition to nearly three thousand lives lost, thousands of people lost their investments and life savings.

My broker was convinced I had gotten some kind of inside information. He wanted to know why I didn't warn him this was going to happen. But I was as shocked and outraged as the rest of the world. I was only obeying the Holy Spirit.

From then on, the dynamics of my prophetic ministry shifted, leaving me in a state of flux. I felt like you do when you bump into furniture after coming out of bright sunlight into a dark room. I prayed and pressed into the Lord. But all I heard was, "I will create in you the ability to see in a whole new way. Your eyes will be remade to recognize my mysteries and wonders, and I will show you how to engage this new paradigm." It was as if I was experiencing spiritual eye surgery. There was no model for it, no precedent that I knew of.

> It is the glory of God to conceal a matter; to search out a matter is the glory of kings.[475]

---

[475] Proverbs 25:2.

So I met with a friend and shared with him what I was hearing from the Lord about entering the workplace as a prophet. I had been taught that "No one who puts a hand to the plow and looks back is fit for service in the kingdom of God,"[476] and I feared that, by entering the workplace, I was turning away from the church and might become unfit for the kingdom.

"When you leave church on Sunday morning," my friend said, "does the Holy Spirit stay behind or does he go with you?"

"He goes with me, since he is in me."

"Exactly. So everywhere you are, the Holy Spirit is with you. So, when do you turn away from the plow?"

That's when the lights went on. How could I have believed that ministry works only in the church? Suddenly I was free to be whatever the Holy Spirit wanted me to be, anywhere, anytime.

I began my new journey with prayer and research. I built a website to make myself available and was shocked when, within a week, I received a call from the human resources department of a Fortune 500 company, asking me to talk to them about a need they had regarding the executive team. The next day I drove five hours to their company headquarters, praying the whole time that the Lord would go before me and prepare the way.

As I drove, the Holy Spirit warned me that the person HR wanted me to minister to would try to intimidate me and rattle my cage. I asked the Lord to prepare me, confident that he would give me the words to say when the time came.

At one point during the meeting with HR, the executive in question rolled his chair over to me and got in my face.

"How the #%@!! do you think you can help me!"

Lord, I prayed, *give me the words.*

---

[476] Luke 9:62.

"I'm going to be a mirror to show you what you look like," I told him, "but you'll be doing all the work."

"Okay," he said, turning to the HR manager, "this is the man."

"Wow!" the manager said after he left, "I've never seen anyone handle him like that, so calm and with such authority."

But I was as surprised as he was.

The Lord continued to give me favor. I worked with this man for nine months, and he was totally transformed by the Holy Spirit. That was the beginning.

I called a friend in Seattle. Steve understood some of the things I was starting to experience and gave me some insight. Then he invited me to a conference where Christian leaders were talking about workplace ministry. From them, and through experience, I've learned that you don't need a degree to consult with business executives. I don't have an MBA, but I do have the Holy Spirit, and he tells me and shows me things that astound them almost as much as they astound me.

Once the leaders of a church in Virginia invited me to minister but cautioned me against ministering in the Holy Spirit. As I shared my testimony, a well-dressed gentleman in the back asked me to pray for him.

"Go ahead," the pastor whispered to me, "but no funny business."

The man walked up, and I reached out to pray for him. But before I even touched him, he hit the floor. The pastor grabbed the microphone and said, "Done."

That man called the next day to tell me he had been healed. He was a U.S. senator, and that's how God opened the door for me to minister to lawmakers in Washington.

That's how things work. You don't hand out business cards that say you're a prophet; you just need to be who you are, wherever you are.

Another time, a company chairman told me, "We have a bunch of fires we have to put out."

"Do you have a fireman in your company?" I asked.

"No," he said.

"Then why are you calling them fires?"

"Because that's what they are."

I explained that he needed to change the way he speaks, because it creates an atmosphere. Instead of calling it a fire, I told him, call it an opportunity, because it is an opportunity to see a demonstration of the goodness of God in the midst of his situation. And if he can see that and speak it and declare it, he'll extend his business with these clients.

He telephoned all his "burning" clients and told me afterward that it had been amazing. Once he changed the way he spoke, it changed the way he thought, which changed what he saw. It changed his expectations, and he was able to communicate reconciliation and restoration instead of showing them the door.

We carry the kingdom of God with us everywhere we go and can impart it to people by the laying on of hands, by speaking and declaring, and by demonstrating, which is far more powerful and productive than preaching.

Where will the Lord lead me next? Judging by another part of the word my friend Vernon prophesied over me back in 1999, just about anywhere.

> I keep seeing that God is even going to change the financial structure of this nation through you, the tax system and the government...
>
> I will cause you to see a place of intercession that few enter into. You will walk into a place of intercession where you know my heart and where

we speak face to face. And I will cause the course of history to be changed...

I break alchemy and mysticism that would try to creep in and the spirit of the sorcerers that would try to creep in...

You will be an advisor...there is a place that God is restoring in the prophetic today like the prophets of old, where you would council kings[477] and leaders of nations. You're entering into that...

When the Lord led me to government officials, I could have camped there and missed many divine appointments in the business sector. Ministering for a while in the business sector, I could have camped and missed a divine appointment that led me into the agricultural sector and another creative miracle.

Remember, I'm just giving you some examples of my experiences in the workplace to give you an idea of what might be ahead.

Once I received a call from a farmer in response to a prophetic dream he had. In the dream, he was told to buy a state-of-the-art tractor and some new harvesting technology and to contact the prophet with the accent that he had seen at one his church meetings. He asked me to come to his farm and bless the land before he planted. So we walked and prayed over the land and the seed in his barn and called forth a bumper crop. As we walked, he slipped an unsolicited check into my hand, explaining that the Lord had instructed him to sow into the prophet.

All went well. The seedlings grew into plants about two feet tall. Then a devastating drought struck the region. He called me, and I returned to his farm. I blessed the ground again and called forth rain, despite the fact that there was none forecast.

I spent the night with him and his family, and when we awoke, it was raining. The rain continued most of the day, and when harvest

---

[477] The destiny of nations is often influenced by international bankers—financial "kings."

time came, he had a massive crop, was able to repay all his debt, and the agricultural bank and a private equity company came and bought the entire operation.

Whether the Holy Spirit sends me to an individual or corporation, to the government or private sector, I just use revelatory intuition to help people make kingdom-minded decisions and become fruitful in their personal lives.

The prophetic in the workplace? God has a lot to reveal to us yet. But I suspect that, when all is said and done, it's going to look pretty much like the prophetic anyplace else.

> 'I will go before you and make the crooked places straight; I will break in pieces the gates of bronze and cut the bars of iron. I will give you the treasures of darkness and hidden riches of secret places, that you may know that I, the LORD, who call *you* by your name, *Am* the God of Israel.[478]

---

[478] Isaiah 45:2-3 NKJV.

CHAPTER TWELVE
the emerging prophet

Sometimes the Holy Spirit works inwardly for almost a
lifetime before that person is given the full platform to
release the message.[479]

~ Mike Bickle

Another function of the prophet is to disciple emerging
prophets. Called prophets arise naturally, like cream. They
are not prophets because they prophesy; they prophesy
because they are prophets. It's not what they do; it's who they are—
who God called, anointed, and equipped them to be.

A man's gift makes room for him and brings him
before great men.[480]

Emerging prophets can be recognized by a number of indicators.
They will generally be attracted to and have an unusual affection for
the Holy Spirit. They will want to encourage leaders and guide the
saints with prophecy and wisdom. They are protective of God's
flock. They often seek the company of mature prophets and try to
glean information about the prophetic. They take the initiative to
learn the fundamentals of the prophetic by studying the Word, the
lives and ministries of biblical prophets, and the writings of
contemporary New Testament prophets.

Also, because they are still immature, they may struggle with a
critical spirit and judgmentalism as they recognize things that are
out of order. They may be intolerant of legalism and religious spirits.

---

[479] Bickle, Mike, with Sullivant, Michael, *Growing in the Prophetic*, Creation House, 1996,
p.82, ISBN: 0-88419-426-4.
[480] Proverbs 18:16 NASB.

207

They are usually not big on gray areas and tend to see everything in black and white. And they tend to be impatient.

These traits do not necessarily indicate that the person is a prophet—the person may just be critical, judgmental, intolerant, myopic, impatient, and antisocial. But they are also characteristics that, through trials and faithfulness, can be transformed into discernment, bearing with the brethren, single-mindedness, patience, and precious fellowship with the Holy Spirit.

In the early days along my prophetic path, I had a real struggle to read and understand Scripture. So I enrolled in night classes at a local Bible college, excited and confident that I was going to become a Bible scholar. But my spirit was grieved at the things the instructors said, things that were simply not scriptural. And when I asked the questions, I was reprimanded and told that I was disrupting the class.

The third night, the teacher returned my check and told me not to come back. I was hurt and on the way home, I said, "Lord, if you want me to be taught about your Word, then send me to someone or send someone to me."

Every Friday, I had been meeting with a pastor friend at my office for tea and a sandwich. One day, about a month after being tossed out of Bible college, something seemed to be bothering him. When I asked him, he told me his church had let him go.

"Hire him," the Lord said. I thought, *he knows nothing about pharmaceuticals. What would he do?* Then I excused myself and went to tell Melanie.

"Well," she said, "if the Lord told you to do so, then do it."

What a novel idea! I returned to my office and said the Lord had told me to hire him.

He was as surprised as I was. Back then I was an if-you-want-it-done-right-do-it-yourself kind of guy, and I didn't have the time or interest in babysitting or training anyone.

"What will I be doing?" he asked.

"I have no idea," I said honestly. "But tomorrow I have to leave on a business trip. Come along, and we'll talk about it."

The next morning, as I drove, he opened his Bible and read a passage to me. Then he began to break it down, and I suddenly understood what the Word was saying. My friend's explanations were clear and precise. This man was God's response to my prayer.

As he did with my friend, God will provide mature prophets to disciple emerging ones. Because, frankly, left to themselves, they can be messy. Ask any pastor who has had one in his community.[481]

Neophyte prophets remind me of a situation that occurred a few years ago at South Africa's Kruger National Park, one of the largest game reserves on the continent. Due largely to poaching, African elephants had become endangered. The herds recovered, but then they grew too large for the reserve. So it was suggested that some of the elephants be helicoptered to Pilanesburg National Park, South Africa's other major game reserve.

The idea was sound and the rigs had no difficulty handling the cows and juvenile males. But the bulls were too much for the harnesses, so they were left behind.

It wasn't long before Pilanesburg Park rangers began finding the bodies of white rhinos, also endangered. Hidden cameras revealed that they were being gored and crushed by the juvenile male elephants from Kruger.

After considerable head scratching, the rangers figured out that the outrageous behavior of the juveniles was due to the absence of the bulls.

> Juvenile male elephants...experience *musth*, a
> state of frenzy triggered by mating season and

---

[481] For an in-depth primer of emerging prophets in the congregation, I recommend *Growing in the Prophetic*, by Mike Bickle, senior pastor of Metro Vineyard Fellowship in Kansas City, Missouri, © 1996, Creation House, Orlando, FL.

increases in testosterone. Normally, dominant bulls manage and contain the testosterone-induced frenzy in the younger males. Left without elephant modeling, the rangers theorized, the younger elephants were missing the civilizing influence of their elders as nature and pachyderm protocol intended.[482]

They reinforced the harnesses, brought in some of the Kruger bull elephants, and the aberrant behavior of the juveniles stopped.

The church, too, is in want of fathers, as is a world in which divorce has become as common as marriage.

> Even if you had ten thousand guardians in Christ, you do not have many fathers, for in Christ Jesus I became your father through the gospel. Therefore I urge you to imitate me.[483]

circle of life

When I was training as a prophet, my discipler systematically built into my life nine biblical principles. It wasn't a nine-step program with the tenth step being graduation. It was a circle of life, a continuing process of being conformed to Christ.

Principle #1 –Identity in Christ

I am a child of God, the beloved of my Father. I am not my gift, talent, attributes, or accomplishments.

> Praise be to the God and Father of our Lord Jesus Christ, who has blessed us in the heavenly realms with every spiritual blessing in Christ. For he chose us in him before the creation of the world to be holy and blameless in his sight. In love he predestined us for adoption to sonship through

---

[482]Retrieved August 9, 2015: http://thesestonewalls.com/gordon-macrae/in-the-absence-of-fathers-a-story-of-elephants-and-men.

[483] 1 Corinthians 4:15-16.

Jesus Christ, in accordance with his pleasure and will—to the praise of his glorious grace, which he has freely given to us in the One he loves.[484]

I learned that all the rejection, self-hate, desperation, and violence in my life was the fruit of an orphan spirit. I was like the little urchins in the movies, dressed in rags, barefoot in the snow, gazing longingly through the restaurant window. I had no one, was no one, belonged nowhere.

One day, I watched the movie *Oliver*, a musical adaptation of the Dickens classic. It's the story of an orphan named Oliver Twist, born and raised in a Victorian workhouse and apprenticed to an undertaker. He escapes to London where he meets the Artful Dodger and joins a gang of young pickpockets led by the reprobate Fagin.

As I watched, I realized that I was like Oliver…until the day my Father found me and brought me into his kingdom. Then he sent Andrew to walk with me day by day and teach me about my Father and my inheritance, to reveal to me my original destiny and start me on the path to the fulfillment of God's promises.

Principle #2 – The Armor of God

> Finally, be strong in the Lord and in the strength of His might. Put on the full armor of God, so that you will be able to stand firm against the schemes of the devil. For our struggle is not against flesh and blood, but against the rulers, against the powers, against the world forces of this darkness, against the spiritual *forces* of wickedness in the heavenly *places*.
>
> Therefore, take up the full armor of God, so that you will be able to resist in the evil day, and having done everything, to stand firm. Stand firm therefore, having girded your loins with truth, and having put on the breastplate of righteousness,

---

[484] Ephesians 1:3-6.

and having shod your feet with the preparation of the gospel of peace; in addition to all, taking up the shield of faith with which you will be able to extinguish all the flaming arrows of the evil *one*.

And take the helmet of salvation, and the sword of the Spirit, which is the word of God. With all prayer and petition pray at all times in the Spirit, and with this in view, be on the alert with all perseverance and petition for all the saints, and *pray* on my behalf, that utterance may be given to me in the opening of my mouth, to make known with boldness the mystery of the gospel...[485]

I was a weapons specialist in the military. If you could shoot something with it, bust something with it, or cut something with it, I could handle it. Throughout my life, I met every threat, challenge, and obstacle with the calm assurance that "I am trained for this."

After I gave my life to Jesus, I had to unlearn all of that. Andrew taught me how to wear my new body armor and trained me to wield far more powerful weapons than anything I had known before.

Principle #3 – Family Relationships

Children, obey your parents in the Lord, for this is right. Honor your father and mother (which is the first commandment with a promise), so that it may be well with you, and that you may live long on the earth. Fathers, do not provoke your children to anger, but bring them up in the discipline and instruction of the Lord. Slaves, be obedient to those who are your masters according to the flesh, with fear and trembling, in the sincerity of your heart, as to Christ...[486]

When you're an orphan, you wouldn't know how to be part of a family if you had one. As Andrew taught me about family

---

[485] Ephesians 6:10-19 NASB.
[486] Ephesians 6:1-5 NASB.

relationships in God's kingdom, the Holy Spirit convicted me of dishonoring my mother and father, both in my heart and to others.

This was preventing me from inheriting God's promise for me, until I repented and asked the Lord's forgiveness. In addition, I asked my parents' forgiveness, even though they had gone on to be with him.

Andrew taught me that it was equally important for me to honor and respect everyone else in authority, both in the church and in secular government.

Principle #4 – Love Your Spouse

This was huge for me. As I said before, in South African culture, wives are not held in very high esteem. But the marriage relationship is very important to God because it is a reflection of his Son's marriage to the church.

> Wives, *be subject* to your own husbands, as to the Lord. For the husband is the head of the wife, as Christ also is the head of the church, He Himself *being* the Savior of the body. But as the church is subject to Christ, so also the wives *ought to be* to their husbands in everything.
>
> Husbands, love your wives, just as Christ also loved the church and gave Himself up for her, so that He might sanctify her, having cleansed her by the washing of water with the word, that He might present to Himself the church in all her glory, having no spot or wrinkle or any such thing; but that she would be holy and blameless.[487]

Andrew taught me that I needed to learn to love my wife as Jesus loves the church and gave himself for her. I don't know how people can function in the prophetic with the right motivation toward the bride of Christ if they do not have a healthy, godly relationship with their spouse.

---

[487] Ephesians 5:22-27 NASB.

Principle #5 – Be Imitators of God

The first four principles shut the doors to the enemy in our lives and arm us against future attacks. Once this is accomplished, we need to turn 180 degrees and fix our eyes on the Lord.

> Therefore be imitators of God, as beloved children; and walk in love, just as Christ also loved you and gave Himself up for us, an offering and a sacrifice to God as a fragrant aroma.[488]

Paul described the kingdom model of leadership in a letter to the church in Corinth.

"Imitate me," he said simply, "just as I imitate Christ."[489]

Principle #6 – The Measure of Christ's Gift

The measure of our gift is determined by our resemblance to the Giver.

We become more like Jesus the better we know him, the more we know about him, and the more clearly we understand his ways. This can include considerable unlearning, some deliverance, and lots of habit breaking.

> So this I say, and affirm together with the Lord, that you walk no longer just as the Gentiles also walk, in the futility of their mind, being darkened in their understanding, excluded from the life of God because of the ignorance that is in them, because of the hardness of their heart; and they, having become callous, have given themselves over to sensuality for the practice of every kind of impurity with greediness.
>
> But you did not learn Christ in this way...[490]

---

[488] Ephesians 5:1-2 NASB.
[489] 1 Corinthians 11:1 AMP.
[490] Ephesians 4:17-20 NASB.

Principle #7 – Unity of the Spirit:

> So I, the prisoner for the Lord, appeal to you to live a life worthy of the calling to which you have been called [that is, to live a life that exhibits godly character, moral courage, personal integrity, and mature behavior—a life that expresses gratitude to God for your salvation], with all humility [forsaking self-righteousness], and gentleness [maintaining self-control], with patience, bearing with one another in [unselfish] love. Make every effort to keep the oneness of the Spirit in the bond of peace [each individual working together to make the whole successful].[491]

Just as we set our eyes on the Father who loves us, the Son of God who redeemed us, and the Holy Spirit who empowers us, we need to keep our focus on the things that unite us: "repentance from dead works and of faith toward God, of the doctrine of baptisms, of laying on of hands, of resurrection of the dead, and of eternal judgment."[492]

Principle # 8 – Being Light

We have been given grace to delve into God's mysteries. And we are anointed to reveal those mysteries to the world, demonstrate the administration of God's kingdom, and show how all his gifts work together in harmony to reveal the truth of Christ and his church.

> To me, the very least of all saints, this grace was given, to preach to the Gentiles the unfathomable riches of Christ, and to bring to light what is the administration of the mystery which for ages has been hidden in God who created all things; so that the manifold wisdom of God might now be made known through the church to the rulers and the authorities in the heavenly *places*.[493]

---

[491] Ephesians 4:1-3 AMP.
[492] Hebrews 6:1-2 NKJV.
[493] Ephesians 3:8-10 NASB.

When Jesus described himself as the way, the truth, and the life,[494] he was not being metaphorical. He does not *have* the way; he *is* the way. He is the truth, not the bearer of truth. And he is life itself. Only in him can we "live and move and have our being."[495]

> It wasn't so long ago that you were mired in that old stagnant life of sin. You let the world, which doesn't know the first thing about living, tell you how to live. You filled your lungs with polluted unbelief, and then exhaled disobedience. We all did it, all of us doing what we felt like doing, when we felt like doing it, all of us in the same boat. It's a wonder God didn't lose his temper and do away with the whole lot of us.
>
> Instead, immense in mercy and with an incredible love, he embraced us. He took our sin-dead lives and made us alive in Christ. He did all this on his own, with no help from us! Then he picked us up and set us down in highest heaven in company with Jesus, our Messiah.
>
> Now God has us where he wants us, with all the time in this world and the next to shower grace and kindness upon us in Christ Jesus. Saving is all his idea, and all his work. All we do is trust him enough to let him do it. It's God's gift from start to finish! We don't play the major role. If we did, we'd probably go around bragging that we'd done the whole thing! No, we neither make nor save ourselves. God does both the making and saving.
>
> He creates each of us by Christ Jesus to join him in the work he does, the good work he has gotten ready for us to do, work we had better be doing.[496]

---

[494] John 14:6.
[495] Acts 17:28.
[496] Ephesians 2:1-10 MSG.

the desert

Emerging prophets also need to be aware that, along the circle of life, they will encounter seasons in the wilderness, referred to by some as the "dark night of the soul."[497]

During these seasons, we may feel that everything has been stripped from us, leaving us with nothing and alone with God. And finding ourselves truly alone and naked before God can be terrifying.

The good news is that we can see God more clearly in the wilderness, just as we can see billions of stars from the desert that are invisible from the city.

We also see ourselves more clearly in the wilderness. The Holy Spirit often brings sins and faults to the surface like dross in gold. When he does, the enemy frequently rushes in to try to turn God's conviction into condemnation to leave us feeling dirty, overwhelmed, even hopeless.

But conviction of sin is just part of God's purification and promotion process. In his incredible love for us, he is saying, "I want you closer to me, but a few things stand in the way. I'm going to turn up the heat a little now to cause the dross to rise to the surface where we can skim it off together. The more we skim, the more like me you will become and the more you will be able to enjoy me."

In the wilderness, an emerging prophet can easily misinterpret what is happening, become discouraged, quit, miss his promotion, and stunt his growth. That's why he needs a "bull elephant" in his life who can teach him what to expect and how much the wilderness can accomplish. As he matures, the prophet even comes to look forward to these intimate times in the desert with the Lover of his soul.

receiving the prophets

When the Holy Spirit began to restore the prophetic to the body of

---

[497] This has become a generic term for a wilderness experience. Originally, it was an eight-stanza poem by 16th century mystic St. John of the Cross, which, while he did not entitle it "Dark night of the soul," chronicles the journey from soulishness to oneness with God.

Christ in the 1980s, things were messy. But as someone said, if you are going to have children, you're going to have poopy diapers. Back then few pastors: a) understood much about the prophetic, or b) had much interest in changing diapers. They didn't know what to do with emerging prophets within their own communities, and the war stories that circulated sent pastors to the battlements when a seasoned prophet came to town.

A few years ago, I got lost on my way to a small town church where I had been invited to minister in the prophetic. I had never met the pastor, I arrived late, and was ushered immediately to the pulpit. I opened my Bible and started to read the Word and pray, when the Holy Spirit stopped me and drew my attention to a man on the right side of the church and a lady on the other side.

I asked them to stand, and the Holy Spirit said to tell them, "Stop what you are doing! This is your final warning!"

The man turned out to be the pastor.

"You are done!" he said, as he lead me out of his church.

I chose not to defend myself or argue. As I left, I said jokingly, "What, no offering?" I can't print his reply. We didn't even talk like that in the military.

A couple of months later, I received a phone call from the elders of that church, repenting of their pastor's behavior. It seems that the lady on the other side of the sanctuary was his secretary, and together they had been charged with stealing money from a retirement community.

Sometimes, the prophetic office is the only one that can deal with things that are out of order. That's why it's vital that emerging prophets be discipled to maturity and released into the body of Christ. It is also vital for the church to have more leaders like Pastor Harold.

"In 2003," he tells friends, "my wife and I were new to many things of the Spirit, especially prophecy. When we attended a conference

218

in East Texas where I was to be ordained, there was a sign-up sheet that would allow you to meet with a prophet for one hour. We had no idea of what to expect. My wife even remarked, 'Wow! This looks like fun.'

"Enter, Ron and Melanie Campbell. This couple had strange accents that caused us to listen intently. At that time, we weren't even aware that people actually operated in the office of prophet.

"We were totally unprepared for their words. We later tried to jot some things down and were in agreement that we wanted to know more of this prophetic thing. We went out on a limb (some call it faith) and invited Ron and Mel to speak at the church. At the time, we had about fifty members.

"That weekend we were blown away by the teaching, the challenges, and especially the ministry time. Many skeptics were skeptics no longer. We began to see God move in agreement with the prophetic word spoken over individuals and over the church.

"I could share many testimonies about how God blessed us as we learned to sow into the prophet, but there was one time in particular that caused us to sit up and take notice.

"As I said, we were a fledgling church, but we were growing. God was blessing us, and we needed more space. We had begun this ministry in 2001. We met wherever we could and saved up for our own building.

"In 2006, we found what we thought was the perfect building downtown. It was a 40,000 square-foot, two-story building, complete with parking. After much prayer and negotiations, we decided to try and borrow the funds to purchase this building. But all our efforts came to a dead end.

"During a leadership meeting at our home, my wife stood up and said, 'Guys, we can't force this to happen. This is going to be a miracle so that God will get the glory.'

"Ron was coming to minister in a couple of weeks. I called him and

219

asked him to pray about the situation, and we left it at that. After our Saturday night service, the four of us went out to dinner.

"On the way into the restaurant, Ron stopped me and said, 'Harold, you asked me to pray about the building. The Lord told me to tell you to let it die.'

"I felt like someone had punched me in the gut. I have to admit I was a little angry at the prophet.

"'But what if the Lord resurrects it?'

"'Then you'll know it was from him and not you.'

"So we did something that Ron said not everyone he ministers to does. We obeyed the word of the Lord. We let it die. We continued to save money for more than a year and met in locations that were either free or cost us very little.

"One day, I received a call from the company that owned the building. A year earlier, they were asking more than $400,000; now they were offering it to us for $100,000! And because we had waited, we had the cash on hand to pay for it in full, with enough left over to start remodeling. We purchased a wonderful building for less than $2.50 per square foot in an area that would soon become the centerpiece of the city. We have been meeting there since Resurrection Day 2008, debt-free, and now have 500 members.

"The building that we paid $98,500 for (we got a refund on pro-rated taxes) is now valued by our insurance company at $5.5 million! With our remodeling, including building a private Christian school, our investment has increased tenfold!"

Like much of the church today, Pastor Harold knew little about the prophetic. But he was teachable. And as a result, he received what Jesus calls the "prophet's reward."

> He who receives *and* welcomes a prophet because
> he is a prophet will receive a prophet's reward;
> and he who receives a righteous (honorable) man

because he is a righteous man will receive a righteous man's reward.[498]

The prophet's reward is simply the fulfillment of the prophetic word.

For example, when Elijah told King Ahab there would be no rain or dew again in Israel until the prophet said so, God promised the prophet he would not go hungry or thirsty.

> The word of the Lord came to him, saying, "Go away from here and turn eastward, and hide yourself by the brook Cherith, which is east of the Jordan. It shall be that you will drink of the brook, and I have commanded the ravens to provide for you there."[499]

One day, the ravens stopped coming and the brook dried up. So, the Lord sent Elijah to find a widow in the town of Zarephath and again promised to provide for him. The widow received Elijah as God's prophet, and, even when he asked her to do what seemed impossible, she followed his instructions.

> …when he came to the gate of the city, behold, a widow was there gathering sticks; and he called to her and said, "Please get me a little water in a jar, that I may drink." As she was going to get *it*, he called to her and said, "Please bring me a piece of bread in your hand." But she said, "As the Lord your God lives, I have no bread, only a handful of flour in the bowl and a little oil in the jar; and behold, I am gathering a few sticks that I may go in and prepare for me and my son, that we may eat it and die."
>
> Then Elijah said to her, "Do not fear; go, do as you have said, but make me a little bread cake from it first and bring *it* out to me, and afterward

---

[498] Matthew 10:41 AMP.
[499] 1 Kings 17:2-4 NASB.

you may make *one* for yourself and for your son. For thus says the Lord God of Israel, 'The bowl of flour shall not be exhausted, nor shall the jar of oil be empty, until the day that the Lord sends rain on the face of the earth.'" So she went and did according to the word of Elijah, and she and he and her household ate for *many* days. The bowl of flour was not exhausted nor did the jar of oil become empty, according to the word of the Lord which He spoke through Elijah.[500]

Elijah obeyed the Lord, and the promise was fulfilled. The widow obeyed the Lord's prophet and received the prophet's reward.

For this reason we also constantly thank God that when you received the word of God which you heard from us, you accepted *it* not *as* the word of men, but *for* what it really is, the word of God, which also performs its work in you who believe.[501]

A no less extraordinary example of receiving the prophet and acting on his word happened in 2004.

I told a young woman that she and her husband were going to have another baby and that the Lord was giving them a prophet. I learned later that the word had come as a big surprise. The couple were very content with their two children and had no plans of having more.

"After the shock wore off," she told me, "I started praying Mary's prayer, 'Lord, be it unto me according to your word.' If this is your will, change my heart."

And he did. She and her husband tried for the next two years to conceive. After her doctor told them she would not be able to conceive naturally, they decided to "help the Lord" by going to a fertility clinic. At the last minute, however, she changed her mind.

---

[500] Ibid., 10-16.
[501] 1 Thessalonians 2:13 NASB.

"Lord," she prayed, "either you are who you say you are, or you're a liar. I'm choosing to believe you are faithful to your word." She sat down with the Bible and asked the Lord for a word of encouragement. The book fell open at Habakkuk 2:2-3.[502]

> Then the LORD answered me and said: "Write the vision and make *it* plain on tablets, that he may run who reads it. For the vision *is* yet for an appointed time; but at the end it will speak, and it will not lie. Though it tarries, wait for it; because it will surely come, it will not tarry.

"From that day forward, I began my real faith walk. I began to war with the word and declare the word over my life." On October 1, 2006, at work, she heard the Lord say Ezekiel 7:12. She wasn't familiar with the verse, so she ran to look it up.

> The time has come, the day draws near.

A month later, she learned she was pregnant. Incredulous, her doctor treated it as a high-risk pregnancy. At around thirteen weeks, she felt a sharp pain and began bleeding. The doctor said if she was going to miscarry, there was nothing he could do.

"I began to war with Psalm 105:15."

> Do not touch my anointed ones and
> do my prophets no harm.

And on July 9, 2007, they became the parents of a healthy (and, undoubtedly, prophetic) baby boy.

> Fight the good fight of the faith. Take hold of the eternal life to which you were called when you made your good confession in the presence of many witnesses.[503]

The prophetic path can be long or short, twist around here and there,

---

[502] NKJV.
[503] 1 Timothy 6:12 NKJV.

lead you over mountains, into valleys, and through deserts. Each path is different, but all prophetic paths lead to an end in the arms of the Christ.

epilogue

The Lord is preparing his church to see things we have never imagined. Our spiritual eyes are being "upgraded" to a higher form of seeing, being remade for greater glory. There's a wonderful picture of this in John's Gospel.

> As he went along, he saw a man blind from birth. His disciples asked him, "Rabbi, who sinned, this man or his parents, that he was born blind?"
>
> "Neither this man nor his parents sinned," said Jesus, "but this happened so that the works of God might be displayed in him. As long as it is day, we must do the works of him who sent me. Night is coming, when no one can work. While I am in the world, I am the light of the world."
>
> After saying this, he spit on the ground, made some mud with the saliva, and put it on the man's eyes. "Go," he told him, "wash in the Pool of Siloam" (this word means "Sent"). So the man went and washed, and came home seeing.[504]

Spitting was frowned upon in Mosaic Law. If a father spat in his daughter's face, she was put to shame for a week.[505] Spitting was a sign of contempt,[506] and an implication of God's disfavor.[507]

But I believe that when Jesus applied the mud to the man's eyes, he performed a creative miracle. Notice that the Bible does not say he

---

[504] John 9:1-7.
[505] Numbers 12:14.
[506] Isaiah 50:6; Matthew 26:67.
[507] Job 17:6.

was healed; it says he could see. I think he received new eyeballs. The saliva from Jesus' mouth contained the DNA of God.

> The Word became flesh and made his dwelling among us. We have seen his glory, the glory of the one and only Son, who came from the Father, full of grace and truth.[508]

The dirt was the element from which man was created.

> Then the Lord God formed a man from the dust of the ground and breathed into his nostrils the breath of life, and the man became a living being.[509]

Jesus mixed God's DNA with the creation element, applied it to the man's eyes, and told him to wash in a pool. And when he emerged from the water, like a newly baptized believer, he could see.

We are all born spiritually blind.

> But the natural man does not receive the things of the Spirit of God, for they are foolishness to him; nor can he know *them,* because they are spiritually discerned.[510]

When we are *re*born, we become a new creation with newly-created eyes.

> Therefore if anyone is in Christ [that is, grafted in, joined to Him by faith in Him as Savior], *he is* a new creature [reborn and renewed by the Holy Spirit]; the old things [the previous moral and spiritual condition] have passed away. Behold, new things have come [because spiritual awakening brings a new life].[511]

---

[508] John 1:14.
[509] Genesis 2:7.
[510] 1 Corinthians 2:14 NKJV.
[511] 2 Corinthians 5:17 AMP.

I love the story in second Kings where the Arameans set one trap after another to destroy Israel. Each time, the prophet Elisha warned Israel's king. Enraged, the king of Aram learned that the prophet was in Dothan and sent his army to kill him.

> When the servant of the man of God got up and went out early the next morning, an army with horses and chariots had surrounded the city. "Oh no, my lord! What shall we do?" the servant asked.
>
> "Don't be afraid," the prophet answered. "Those who are with us are more than those who are with them."
>
> And Elisha prayed, "Open his eyes, Lord, so that he may see." Then the Lord opened the servant's eyes, and he looked and saw the hills full of horses and chariots of fire all around Elisha.[512]

New eyes, however, are of little use if we keep them shut. We need to open them to supernatural opportunities outside our expectations.

So where do you go from here?

Into the world, into the church, wherever and whenever the Holy Spirit leads you. He is your Teacher and your Guide and the only Source of your power.

The Holy Spirit is our school of the prophets.

> As for you, the anointing you received from him remains in you, and you do not need anyone to teach you. But as his anointing teaches you about all things and as that anointing is real, not counterfeit—just as it has taught you, remain in him.[513]

---

[512] vv. 15-17.
[513] 1 John 2:27.

> For His divine power has bestowed
> on us [absolutely] everything
> necessary for [a dynamic spiritual]
> life and godliness, through true *and*
> personal knowledge of Him who
> called us by His own glory and
> excellence.[514]

> Do not merely listen to the word, and
> so deceive yourselves. Do what it
> says.[515]

> Calling the Twelve to him, he began
> to send them out two by two and gave
> them authority over impure spirits.[516]

You are unique. You cannot tailor your gift and calling to look like mine or anyone else's. No man can teach you how to be the you the Holy Spirit has destined you to be. This book, as the name suggests, is a prophetic path. The end of the book is your jumping off place *into* the prophetic. Yes, the Holy Spirit will send men and women throughout your life who will illuminate and impact your life, and you will have close relationships.

> From him the whole body, joined and
> held together by every supporting
> ligament, grows and builds itself up in
> love, as each part does its work.[517]

But the most important relationship—the one with whom to begin and end every day and to walk with and talk with throughout each day—is the Holy Spirit, your Default, your Factory Setting, your God and your Best and Dearest Friend.

So go with God, my friend. And don't look back.

---

[514] 2 Peter 1:3 AMP.
[515] James 1:22.
[516] Mark 6:7.
[517] Ephesians 4:16.

RON CAMPBELL

 Ron Campbell was born in Johannesburg, South Africa. He served with the South African Defense Force as a specialist in tactical warfare.

This experience provided him with a unique perspective on building and equipping teams, strategic skills he now employs to develop effective, long-term performance in the corporate world. Following his military service, Ron built a multinational pharmaceutical business.

The Holy Spirit led Ron to America in 1993 to minister life and transformation in the office of a prophet. He has been used powerfully by the Lord, ministering healing and building up believers through words of knowledge and words of wisdom.

Ron's clients include the Texas legislature, U.S. Senate and House of Representatives, and Life Care Medical Foundation, as well as oil corporations, technology companies, nongovernment organizations, and churches.

Ron is also a popular and engaging conference, seminar, and keynote speaker.

Sound the Trumpet Ministries International, Inc.[518]
P O Box 188
Grapevine, TX 76099-0188

---

[518] Sound the Trumpet Ministries is an international Christian ministry founded to equip and encourage people to enter their God-ordained purpose, serve as ambassadors of the kingdom of God, and positively affect their sphere of influence for God's glory.

RON BRACKIN

Ron Brackin has authored and ghostwritten more than twenty-five books, including the international bestseller, *Son of Hamas*, and traveled extensively in the Middle East and North Africa as an investigative journalist.

Ron also has contributed articles and columns to many publications, including *USA Today* and *The Washington Times*.

He was a broadcast journalist with the all-news CBS radio station in Washington D.C. and served as a congressional press secretary during the Reagan Administration.

More Books by Ron Brackin:

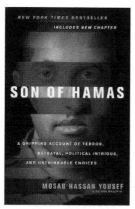

Son of Hamas is now available with an all-new chapter about events since the book's release such as the revelation of Mosab's Israeli intelligence handler's true identity, and Homeland Security's effort to deport the author. Since he was a small boy, Mosab Hassan Yousef has had an inside view of the deadly terrorist group Hamas. The oldest son of Sheikh Hassan Yousef, a founding member of Hamas and its most popular leader, young Mosab assisted his father for years in his political activities while being groomed to assume his legacy, politics, status...and power. But everything changed when Mosab turned away from terror and violence, and embraced instead the teachings of another famous Middle East leader. In *Son of Hamas*, Mosab reveals new information about the world's most dangerous terrorist organization and unveils the truth about his own role, his agonizing separation from family and homeland, the dangerous decision to make his newfound faith public, and his belief that the Christian mandate to "love your enemies" is the only way to peace in the Middle East.

People who forgive live healthier and longer and have better marriages than people who don't. Corporate executives who train their employees to forgive waste less money than those who don't. Nations and ethnic groups that learn to forgive stop trying to destroy one another. So, why do employers still lose billions of dollars to petty squabbles in the marketplace? Why are Palestinians and Israelis still killing one another? Why do millions of people still suffer needlessly from stress-related sicknesses and infirmities caused by unforgiveness? Because we lack understanding and courage. The purpose of this little book is to remove one of those obstacles.

Nevermore to Die is an adventure/thriller, set in the Middle East. It's filled with international intrigue, archeologists and terrorists, healers and demons—all in a deadly race to unearth the historic Tree of Life in the Garden of Eden. And seize immortality! Only one tiny nation stands in their way...

Iraq ... Assyria ... Babylon! Call it what you will. You'll never see it the same way again! From Cain and Abel to Shock & Awe, Iraq may well be the most violent nation on earth. Yet, God calls it his "handiwork" and declares that, along with Egypt and Israel, it will bless the earth. Track Iraq through Scripture, from Genesis to Revelation! Meet Iraqi Christians! Look past the headlines and see what God sees!

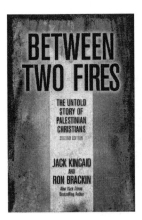

Palestinian Christians...rejected by Palestinians because they won't take up arms against Israel. Rejected by Israelis because they're Palestinian. Rejected by the historical church because they're evangelical. Rejected by the West because, well, all Palestinians are terrorists, aren't they? For the first time, they get to tell their story—uncut and untempered by political correctness. More stories you'll never see on CNN—stories that will amaze you and touch your heart!

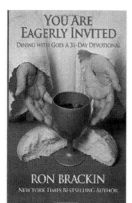

Encouraged by his pastor to share the Lord's Supper more frequently—at home, at work, wherever and whenever—Ron Brackin set out to have an adventure with God. And now, he invites you to come along. Known mostly for the NYT bestseller "Son of Hamas" and his books on the church in the Middle East, Ron leads his readers on a delightful new journey deep into the kingdom of God. But be warned: you may not want to stop at the end of thirty-one days.

Christianity is a roller coaster ride. Whoever says it ain't, don't got a ticket. One day, you're toppling Philistines like ten-pins. Next day, you're hiding in a cave, surrounded by 400 losers. Like David—and every Christian who ever took Jesus for better or worse, richer or poorer, in sickness and in health, Ron Brackin has his ups and downs, expressed herein in 86 bits of verse.

God can be found anywhere - even on a dark and stormy night, amidst the cobwebs and coffins of Castle Dracula. "Dracula - a devotional" includes the entire text of Bram Stoker's timeless horror classic. After each of the 27 chapters is a personal devotion to help readers deepen their intimacy with Jesus Christ and better navigate the Kingdom of God. This enlightening and enjoyable devotional is best enjoyed beside a reassuring fire, with a nice cup of tea...and, perhaps, just a small clove of garlic. The first volume of The Gospel According to the Classics series.

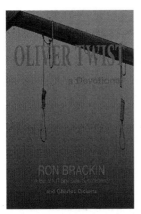

It includes the entire text of Charles Dickens' classic story of mystery and mischief, murder, madness, and munificence - set amidst the squalor and splendor of not-so-jolly Victorian England...and in the shadow of the gallows. After each of the 53 chapters is a personal devotional to help readers deepen their intimacy with Jesus Christ and better navigate the Kingdom of God. This enlightening and provocative devotional is best enjoyed beside a comfortable fire on a dark and stormy night with a nice cup of tea. Volume two of The Gospel According to the Classics series.

Fascinated by the drama of obsessive hatred or narcissistic betrayal? Read Shakespeare. Enjoy curling up on a dark and stormy night with a tale of mystery, murder, and mayhem? Bill's your man. Delight in fairies and ghosts, witches and magic...adore the pomp and pageantry of courts and castles? I say again, read Shakespeare. And now one of Shakespeare's most pleasant—and least bawdy or bloody—plays, is also a devotional—volume three of The Gospel According to the Classics series. "The Annotated Much Ado About Nothing" includes the entire original script, with the added feature of a personal devotional at the end of each of the 17 scenes. This delightful and enlightening devotional is best enjoyed on a full stomach, after roast lamb, funnel cakes, and spiced mead.

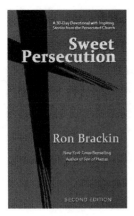

When was the last time you heard a sermon on the theology of suffering? Maybe never. Yet, persecution and suffering are as much a part of the normal Christian life as prayer, worship, and Bible study. But can it ever be "sweet." Only those who have walked through the fires hand in hand with Jesus can answer that. Their experiences will help you get above the suffering in your life. This powerful little devotional is filled with true testimonies from the persecuted church that will strengthen, encourage, and inspire you and help you be even more of a blessing to others.

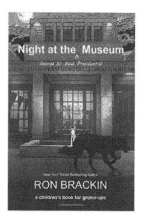

"Someday, you will be old enough to start reading fairy tales again." ~ C.S. Lewis Finally, a children's book for grown-ups! A museum is not a mausoleum where the Past is entombed. A museum is a world filled with wonders. And sometimes, a museum is even an adventure, where, after the sun goes down, the lights are turned off, and the doors are locked, the slumbering Past springs to its feet.

Before 221b Baker Street, young Sherlock Holmes lodged in his rooms at Christ Church, Oxford. Before Dr. John H. Watson, Holmes was accompanied in his adventures by his college don, Rev. Charles Dodgson, aka Lewis Carroll (yes, Alice's Lewis Carroll). And before the tin dispatch box with its trove of unpublished adventures, there was discovered, in an old leather document case, a most unusual manuscript, published now for the first time. Be prepared to enter the dark underworld of Victorian London - Seven Dials, Billingsgate, and the waterfront! A world peopled with murderers and magicians, royalty and rogues! A series of jewel thefts suddenly turns to murder. And Holmes and Dodgson are led from an old English manor through a magician's workshop beneath the mysterious Egyptian Hall to one of her majesty's most closely guarded secrets. "Sherlock Holmes and The Adventure of the Deadly Illusion" is Victorian mystery at its tastiest. "As nineteenth-century specialist, I found it wonderfully evocative of that period. I found the prison sermon spellbinding..." ~ La Donna Flagg, Honor Books

Made in the USA
Middletown, DE
19 March 2018